Comments on other *Amazing Stories* from readers & reviewers

*"Tightly written volumes filled with lots of wit and humour about famous and infamous Canadians."*
Eric Shackleton, *The Globe and Mail*

*"The heightened sense of drama and intrigue, combined with a good dose of human interest is what sets* Amazing Stories *apart."*
Pamela Klaffke, *Calgary Herald*

*"This is popular history as it should be... For this price, buy two and give one to a friend."*
Terry Cook, a reader from Ottawa, on **Rebel Women**

*"Glasner creates the moment of the explosion itself in graphic detail...she builds detail upon gruesome detail to create a convincingly authentic picture."*
Peggy McKinnon, *The Sunday Herald*, on **The Halifax Explosion**

*"It was wonderful...I found I could not put it down. I was sorry when it was completed."*
Dorothy F. from Manitoba on **Marie-Anne Lagimodière**

*"Stories are rich in description, and bristle with a clever, stylish realness."*
Mark Weber, *Central Alberta Advisor*, on **Ghost Town Stories II**

*"A compelling read. Bertin...has selected only the most intriguing tales, which she narrates with a wealth of detail."*
Joyce Glasner, *New Brunswick Reader*, on **Strange Events**

*"The resulting book is one readers will want to share with all the women in their lives."*
Lynn Martel, *Rocky Mountain Outlook*, on **Women Explorers**

# CHRISTMAS IN ATLANTIC CANADA

# AMAZING STORIES

# CHRISTMAS IN ATLANTIC CANADA

Heartwarming Legends, Tales, and Traditions

HOLIDAY

by Joyce Glasner

PUBLISHED BY ALTITUDE PUBLISHING CANADA LTD.
1500 Railway Avenue, Canmore, Alberta  T1W 1P6
www.altitudepublishing.com
1-800-957-6888

Extreme care has been taken to ensure that all information presented in
this book is accurate and up to date. Neither the author nor the
publisher can be held responsible for any errors.

Publisher        Stephen Hutchings
Associate Publisher    Kara Turner
Series Editor    Jill Foran
Editor    Deborah Lawson

We acknowledge the financial support of the Government
of Canada through the Book Publishing Industry Development
Program (BPIDP) for our publishing activities.

**Altitude GreenTree Program**
Altitude Publishing will plant twice as many trees as were used
in the manufacturing of this product.

We acknowledge the support of the Canada Council for the Arts which
in 2003 invested $21.7 million in writing and publishing throughout Canada.

Canada Council    Conseil des Arts
for the Arts    du Canada

**National Library of Canada Cataloguing in Publication Data**

Glasner, Joyce
Christmas in Atlantic Canada / Joyce Glasner.

(Amazing stories)
Includes bibliographical references.
ISBN 1-55153-781-8

1. Christmas--Maritime Provinces. I. Title. II. Series: Amazing stories (Canmore, Alta.)


GT4987.15.G53 2004        394.2663'09715        C2004-903754-4

An application for the trademark for Amazing Stories™
has been made and the registered trademark is pending.

Printed and bound in Canada by Friesens
2  4  6  8  9  7  5  3  1

In loving memory of my mother, Shirley Glasner.
And for my father, Ronald Glasner

# Contents

# Prologue

*They were nearing Moncton when they rounded a corner and the Chrysler began to fishtail wildly across the snow-covered highway. Liam Warner's pulse raced. He gripped the steering wheel tighter and eased up on the gas pedal. The highway was barely visible through the driving snow. Once the car was back under control, he glanced over at his friend in the passenger seat. Allen Morton flashed him a nervous grin and then looked at the red cooler in the back seat.*

*It had been about 10 p.m. on December 15, 2003, when Liam Warner and Allen Morton left Saint John Regional Hospital carrying the red, soft-sided cooler with "ORGANS FOR TRANSPLANT" stencilled on its side. Nested in ice inside the cooler were two kidneys destined for a transplant recipient in Halifax. Since the blizzard had grounded all flights in and out of Saint John, the hospital had appealed to a local cab company for help in delivering the precious cargo.*

*Twenty-five-year-old Liam Warner had just returned to his cab after delivering groceries to a shut-in when the dispatcher's voice crackled over the radio. "Do I have a car willing to take a delivery from Saint John Regional to Halifax tonight?" the dispatcher asked. Warner had made that run the week before with a supply of blood, so he knew the drill.*

Christmas in Atlantic Canada

*He didn't think twice before responding. Once the dispatcher gave him the details, Warner called his wife to let her know he wouldn't be home that night. Then he called his friend Morton and asked if he was up for a wild trip to Halifax.*

*The two men were in high spirits as they set out on their journey. Once they were underway, however, Warner realized the roads were much more treacherous than he'd anticipated. The storm was so bad that the only other vehicles still on the road were a few transport trucks. As they crawled along through whiteout after whiteout, the cabbie grew increasingly anxious. He'd witnessed a bad accident along this same route the week before. One slip and they could end up in the same situation. He was determined to make the delivery and get back home in one piece. After all, Christmas was just around the corner and he was looking forward to spending the holiday with his family.*

*Conditions through Cobequid Pass were so bad that Warner began to worry they might not make it. The wipers, heavily crusted with snow, were all but useless. He had to strain to see anything up ahead. A faint track where a truck had passed through a short time before was all that was visible in the sea of white. Warner hunched over the wheel and followed the track.*

*After seven harrowing hours on the road, Warner and Morton finally arrived in Halifax. They made their way through the silent, pre-dawn streets to the hospital, where a team of surgeons was standing by. "You're right on time!" a*

12

## Prologue

*lab technician exclaimed as he saw the cabbie come striding through the doors. A rush of elation surged through Warner as he handed over the red cooler and headed back out into the cool morning air.*

*Chapter 1*

# Customs and Legends of the Holiday Season

hristmas just wouldn't be Christmas without the myths, rituals, and traditions that give the holiday its special flavour. Throughout the centuries, some of the most colourful customs of the season, from mumming to hunting the wren, have been observed right here in Atlantic Canada.

### The Twelve Days of Christmas

Although the Twelve Days of Christmas are all but obsolete today, they were once a vital and significant part of Atlantic Canada's Christmas season. In fact, just about every other tradition of the season is somehow connected to these twelve days. It was during the Twelve Days of Christmas, for example, that the tree was put up (and taken down again), the Yule log was lit, the mummers went mumming and the belsnicklers belsnickling.

The Twelve Days of Christmas, which fall between December 25 and January 6, were first instituted in the sixth century. In those early days of Christianity, Church leaders were eager to convert as many pagans as possible. One way of doing this, they reasoned, was to replace pagan festivals and feast days with Christian ones. For several centuries prior to the birth of Christ, the weeks between December 21 and January 6 had always been a time for celebration. From the commemoration of the rebirth of the sun during the winter solstice, to the Germanic festival of Yule (which marked the passing of the old year and beginning of the new), these two weeks were filled with great ritual and ceremony. So it was no small coincidence that church leaders chose December 25 as the date of the Nativity and January 6 as the Epiphany, with various saint's days filling up the calendar in between. By superimposing their own holidays on those of ancient pagan feast days, Church leaders not only eased the transition from paganism to Christianity, they also created the much-loved Twelve Days of Christmas.

During the Victorian era, the Twelve Days of Christmas were packed with solemn church services, festive parties, and lavish balls. And in Halifax in the 1850s, the biggest social event of the year was the Twelfth Night ball at Government House.

In 1853, an 18-year-old socialite named Sarah Clinch recorded the events leading up to that dazzling event in her diary. On December 24 she wrote: "We have received an invitation to the Uniacke's [Attorney General Richard John Uniacke] next Thursday and another to an 'At Home' at Government House on Twelfth Night. It is on Twelfth Night that the ring is drawn for. I wish I could get it. It is worth ten dollars and whoever draws it opens the ball with the Governor."

For the next twelve days, Sarah recorded all of her daily activities — the visiting, the dances, the church services, the shopping, and most importantly, the preparations for the ball on Twelfth Night. Her anticipation is palpable in the detailed descriptions of what she planned to wear and how she would do her hair for the event. On January 5 she wrote: "... I am to have my hair flattened tonight at Mrs. Moren's to try the effect and if it is good, I will wear it to Government House tomorrow." She also daydreamed about who would be there and, more importantly, with whom she would dance. "As it is to be the only 'At Home' at the house for the season, it will be very large and there will be no ring ... Charlie Almon is going to take a pencil to Government House tomorrow for me to write down the names of my dancing partners as I forgot this evening once I was engaged to him. He has engaged me for the second quadrille tomorrow evening."

Finally, the highly anticipated day arrived: "Jan. 6. Twelfth Night. I was so tired that I had to lie down this afternoon so as to be able to go to Government House tonight." That evening, Sarah would have been resplendent in her new gown, a gauzy, elaborate creation, which she and the seamstress had worked on for hours that week. "My dress will be Indian muslin double skirt with three rows of narrow satin ribbon on each skirt, breadth of crepe and ribbon flowers in my bosom," she wrote. "And a very pretty wreath in my hair which will be braided behind and curled in front."

It was a fairytale evening, with Sarah and her cousin Miriam being escorted to the ball by "the Chipman's." Government House was undoubtedly decked out in garlands of greenery with a lavishly decorated Christmas tree in the main ballroom, but the 18-year-old was far too busy floating around the dance floor to pay much attention to the decorations. As she later wrote with satisfaction, "I danced every quadrille and was engaged for six more, when the ball broke up."

### The Yule Log

In the past, the Twelve Days of Christmas usually began with a bang in Atlantic Canada. Once the Yule log was lit on Christmas Eve, people would step outside and fire a few shots into the air, marking the beginning of the festive season.

Fire has always been an essential part of winter solstice rituals, so it makes sense that the lighting and burning of the Yule log was once a significant symbolic ritual throughout the western world. The quest for the Yule log was usually a family affair. Every year, the whole family went out in search of just the right tree from which to cut the log. It was believed that bad luck would befall the household if the burning log happened to go out before January 6. Therefore, only the largest log available was chosen.

After the right log was selected, it was brought into the home, placed on the hearth, and lit with a burning piece of wood, or "brand," saved from the previous year's log. Keeping the brand from one year to the next was symbolic of an eternal flame, or passing of the fire. Once lit, the Yule log had to be carefully attended. In addition to the fear of it going out, homeowners also had to worry about the log being consumed too quickly. To ensure it didn't burn out before the allotted time, the Yule log was usually placed on the back of the fireplace grate, where it would smoulder away throughout the Twelve Days.

**Mummers and Belsnicklers**

Perhaps the most colourful tradition connected to the Twelve Days of Christmas is mumming. This ancient custom of dressing up in costumes and parading through the streets began in Europe in the Middle Ages. The tradition is believed to have sprung from the Romans' Saturnalia festival. Brought to Newfoundland with the first English and Irish settlers, mumming became a popular form of entertainment among the working class during the Christmas season. Members of the upper class, however, abhorred the practice. They felt mumming was a crass form of entertainment, and that mummers were no better than everyday hooligans.

There were two forms of mumming in Newfoundland. In the urban areas, mummers paraded through the streets, while those in the outlying areas usually went door to door like children at Halloween. By the mid-19th century, the rowdy antics of the mummers, or "Jannies" as they were known in some areas, had gotten completely out of hand. Throughout the Twelve Days of Christmas, large gangs of mummers would parade through the narrow streets of St. John's led by a hobbyhorse. Wearing masks, outrageous hats, and white shirts bedecked with hundreds of coloured ribbons, the mummers cavorted after the hobbyhorse, mocking and harassing those who gathered to watch the spectacle. Many mummers carried small bags of flour, or "bladders" filled with pebbles, which they pelted at the innocent bystanders. Some even carried whips, with which they threatened those not in costumes. Occasionally, the mummers performed a play involving characters such as Saint George, the Grand Turk, a doctor, and others. But more often than not they just acted up.

On December 28, 1861, the situation reached a breaking point in Bay Roberts. That day, Isaac Mercer and his two brothers-in-law were making their way home after a long day's work in the woods when they spied a group of men wearing grotesque masks heading in their direction. Before Mercer and his companions knew it, the mummers had surrounded them. The masked men drunkenly taunted Mercer and his companions, and a brawl broke out. Mercer was the first to hit the ground. In a frenzy, the masked men fell upon him, kicking and beating him until he stopped struggling. Fearing they may have killed him, the mummers staggered off into the darkness.

After picking Mercer up and carrying him home, his companions fetched the doctor. Once he had examined the victim, the doctor reluctantly informed Mercer's young wife that her husband's skull was fractured. There was little that could be done for him. Tragically, Isaac Mercer died early the following morning.

The vicious beating death of Isaac Mercer shocked the people of Newfoundland. The fact that the attackers had been disguised in their mumming costumes and couldn't be identified sent a chill through the population of Bay Roberts and beyond. The public outcry against mumming reached a fevered pitch. And on June 25, 1861, an act outlawing the tradition was passed. The act, "to Make Further Provision for the Prevention of Nuisances," declared that, "Any person who shall be found at any season of the year, in any Town or Settlement in this colony, without a written licence from the Magistrate, dressed as a Mummer, masked or otherwise disguised, shall be deemed to be guilty of a Public Nuisance, and may be arrested by any Peace Officer..." If found guilty of the crime, the offender would be "committed to Gaol for a Period not exceeding Seven Days" or fined up to 20 shillings, which was about a week's wages for the average person at the time.

Still, despite the ban, the custom lived on in rural communities. Today, "going out in the mummers" is still practised in many parts of Newfoundland during the Christmas season. Beginning on December 26, men and women dress up in costumes and travel from house to house knocking on doors. When the door is opened, the question, "Any mummers 'llowed in tonight?" is posed in "mummer talk," which consists of disguising the voice by using ingressive speech. Once inside, the mummers amuse their hosts by dancing, singing, and talking mummer talk. They remain in disguise until the hosts guess their identities. Then the masks come off and refreshments are served.

In Lunenburg County, Nova Scotia, the ritual of dressing in costumes and going door to door at Christmas is known as belsnickling. Like mummers, belsnicklers wear masks to disguise their identities. There are a few different theories about the origin of the word "belsnickling." One theory suggests that it sprang from the fact that the men used to dress up in ox hides and wear bells around their necks when they went out on their rounds. A more likely theory is that "belsnickles" was an abbreviation of "The Bells of Saint Nicholas." Belsnicklers frequently carry musical instruments on their rounds and entertain their hosts with a musical performance before being served refreshments.

Many in Lunenburg County feel that belsnickling is one

of the best things about the holiday season. Ron Barkhouse of New Ross remembers the thrill of getting dressed up and going out belsnickling with his cousins back in the 1930s and 40s. "The main objective," he says, "was to disguise your identity."

The belsnicklers' costumes are usually quite simple. Often they consist of nothing more than a fisherman's scallop bag or a paper bag (with eyeholes cut out) covering the head, and some old clothes (usually those of the opposite sex). Some belsnicklers, however, are a little more creative in their costume designs. Barkhouse remembers a man coming to his door one year dressed as a house, his head concealed in a cardboard box painted up to look like a chimney!

**Hunting the Wren**

Like mumming, the hunting of the wren also came to Newfoundland with the early settlers. Until late in the 19th century in many parts of Newfoundland, packs of boys marched from house to house with a dead wren attached to a pole topped with greenery and ribbons on St. Stephen's Day (Boxing Day). As they paraded through the streets, the boys would sing, "The wren, the wren, / The king of all birds, / On St. Stephen's Day / Is caught in the furze."

This curious ritual is another example of the residual influence of ancient paganism on this holiday season. Pagans held the wren in high esteem, calling it the "King of all Birds." It was believed that since the wren was so mighty, its ritualistic sacrifice would appease the gods, guaranteeing good luck for the coming year. Though the Christian Church frowned upon it, the custom somehow survived into the 20th century. However, in later years, a facsimile often replaced the actual wren.

## Talking Animals

In one way or another, animals have always been an important part of Christmas in Atlantic Canada. In the Eastern Passage area of Nova Scotia, folks tell the tale of the Christmas when one of the locals was frightened to death by his team of oxen. It was around midnight one Christmas Eve when the old man happened into the barn and overheard his oxen having a conversation. Word has it that one oxen said to the other: "This time tomorrow we'll be hauling wood for our master's coffin." Overcome with fright at this astonishing occurrence, the old man keeled over and died right on the spot.

The myth of animals miraculously being endowed with the gift of human speech at the stroke of midnight on Christmas Eve is still believed by many throughout the Maritime Provinces. It is said that at midnight, oxen and cows in the manger will sink to their knees and begin talking. But if a person should happen to overhear their conversation, he or she won't live to see the next Christmas. This myth, which has been passed on for centuries, has a number of variations. One version tells of people being struck blind when they attempt to witness the miraculous occurrence. Others suggest the cows don't actually speak, but sink to their knees and low in adoration, just as they did in Bethlehem the night that Christ was born.

**The Yuletide Tree**
One custom that was practiced in Halifax during the Victorian era included animals in the celebrations in an interesting manner. During the Christmas season in the late 1800s, a special "Yuletide tree" was erected at the foot of George Street in downtown Halifax. Rather than being decorated with the usual strings of cranberries, popcorn, and glass ornaments, however, this tree had apples and containers of oats dangling from its branches. The fruit and grain were special Christmas treats for the many cabbie horses that spent their days and nights hauling fares up and down the cobblestone streets of the city. On Christmas Eve, the cabbies would take their horses to the Yuletide tree for their Christmas treat. Once motorized vehicles replaced horses as the main mode of transportation, the custom died out. But in 1960, some 55 years after it had disappeared, the tradition was revived. This time, the treats on the Yuletide tree weren't for horses, but for the birds.

Like most things, Christmas customs and rituals are constantly changing to reflect society's values. Many traditions that were once a significant part of the holiday season have gradually died out, or have been replaced by new customs. For example, Atlantic Canadians no longer hunt the wren at Christmas; instead, they honour animals by featuring them in live nativity scenes and processions. Of course, there are some holiday traditions — such as mumming and bel-snickling — that have changed very little over the centuries, and these will likely remain a part of the Christmas season for many years to come.

# Chapter 2
# Memorable Maritime Christmases

rom the first Christmas celebrated by Europeans in a permanent settlement in Canada, to the great Christmas blizzard of 1970, Atlantic Canada's past is filled with historic events, large and small, which have occurred during the holiday season.

## The First Noel

One of the first Christmases celebrated by Europeans in Canada took place in 1604 on Isle Ste. Croix on the border between New Brunswick and Maine. There, French fur trader Pierre du Gua de Monts, explorer Samuel de Champlain, and 120 men — including skilled labourers, a priest, and a minister — set up the first French colony in Acadia, the region extending from Pennsylvania to Cape Breton, Nova Scotia.

## Memorable Maritime Christmases

Compared to the lavish celebrations they were used to back in France, that first Christmas in the New World must have seemed dismal to the settlers.

After searching for a suitable location for several weeks, Champlain and his companions finally settled on the island in June of 1604. At first it seemed the ideal place for the settlement. Its location made it easy to defend and its beauty made it a pleasant haven in the foreign wilderness. The group spent the summer clearing the land, building houses, and planting gardens. By the time winter set in, they felt they were quite prepared for it. But the severity of that first winter exceeded all expectations.

"Winter came upon us sooner than expected, and prevented us from doing many things which we had proposed," Champlain later recorded in his journal. It began to snow early in October and continued almost non-stop for the rest of the winter. By early December, the river was choked with ice, making it all but impossible to leave the island. Since the men had stripped the island of most of the trees in order to build their settlement, they had little fuel left for heating. In addition, there was a serious shortage of clean drinking water. As Champlain wrote: "We were obliged to use very bad water, and drink melted snow, as there were no springs nor brooks." Worse still, with the exception of some Spanish wine and cider, their entire supply of liquors froze.

The place that had seemed so idyllic in summer had become a frigid, inhospitable prison by Christmastime.

Samuel de Champlain

And although the men had plenty of salted meat and fish to eat, they had little in the way of fruits and vegetables. Malnourished and freezing, many of the settlers began to come down with what Champlain called the "mal de terre," or scurvy. At one point, 59 of the men suffered from the dreaded disease. By spring, 35 had succumbed to it.

*Memorable Maritime Christmases*

Although there is no record of how Champlain and his companions spent Christmas that first year, undoubtedly it would have been a highlight in that otherwise miserable winter on Isle Ste. Croix. The colony's priest and minister would have performed Christmas services in the little chapel. Special dishes such as pigeon pie, stew, and baked squash may have been prepared for the Christmas dinner. And no doubt some of the precious Spanish wine would have been used to toast their first Christmas in the new world.

Somehow, the colonists managed to survive that inaugural winter, and in the spring they set out in search of a more suitable location for the settlement. Two years later, Champlain, de Monts, and the others were settled into the first permanent colony in North America at Port Royal, in what is now Nova Scotia. Although conditions had improved dramatically from those endured that first winter, there was little to keep the men entertained during the long, dark winter evenings. Morale began to lag.

In order to alleviate the tedium of the winter months, Champlain came up with the notion of a social club of sorts, which he named *L'Ordre de Bon Temps*, or the "Order of Good Cheer." The idea was that each day a different chief steward was appointed to oversee the evening's meal and entertainment. The Order of Good Cheer was an instant success. Shortly after its inception, the men began competing to see who could provide the best meat, game, fish, and other delicacies for the feasts. In his *History of New France*, poet

and historian Marc Lescarbot described the pomp and cir-
cumstance involved in these nightly feasts: "The ruler of the
feast or chief butler ... marched in, napkin on shoulder, wand
of office in hand, and around his neck the collar of the Order,
which was worth more than four crowns; after him all the
members of the Order, carrying each a dish. The same was
repeated at dessert, though not always with so much pomp."
After the meal was over, the collar of the Order was passed
to the next day's chief steward. And the evening ended with
the outgoing and incoming stewards drinking a toast to
one another.

Christmas at Port Royal that year would have been a
festive affair. The long, low-ceilinged dining room may have
been festooned with evergreen boughs and filled with fire-
light and music. Special dishes such as roast venison, rab-
bit stew, squash, and bread would have been washed down
with copious amounts of wine and spirits. And guests, such
as Mi'kmaw Chief Henry Membertou and others, may have
been invited to join the colonists for the Christmas feast that
year. The French held Chief Membertou in high regard. They
were indebted to the Mi'kmaq, who not only supplied the
settlers with fresh meat, but also taught them how to survive
in the hostile environment. So, inviting them to this special
celebration would have been an appropriate way for the
French to show their gratitude.

## Acadian Christmas

A little over a century after Samuel de Champlain and Pierre du Gua de Monts started the first permanent settlement in Acadia, the British overthrew the French to become the reigning power throughout much of the Maritime region. However, France still had a toehold in the area at Fortress Louisbourg, in what is now Cape Breton. That, combined with the fact that the Acadian population remaining in the region after the takeover outnumbered the English three to one, made the British nervous. Fearing an uprising, they demanded that all Acadians swear an oath of allegiance to the British Crown. The Acadians feared that signing the oath would mean they'd be forced to take up arms against their own people in the event of war with France. As a result of this concern, most refused to sign. They were a peaceful, agricultural society and wanted to remain neutral.

In 1755, the Acadians were again pressed to sign an oath of allegiance to the British. This time when they refused, the British decided once and for all to rid themselves of these "bad subjects." The expulsion of the Acadians began in September of 1755. Acadians throughout the region were rounded up, their property and livestock were confiscated, and their homes, churches, and schools were torched. The British planned to force the Acadians onto ships and transport them to various points all down the eastern seaboard. The idea, no doubt, was to scatter them in small pockets so they would be less likely to reunite and return en masse. The embarkation began the following month. Men, women, and children were herded like cattle onto dozens of overcrowded ships. Many were separated from families and loved ones, some never to see each other again.

The gruelling journey south took up to three months, and conditions aboard the ships were appalling. Overcrowding, scant provisions, and bad water caused illness among the passengers. Many died before reaching their destination. Those who survived the journey found themselves destitute and thousands of miles from home that December. Christmas must have been a miserable affair for all Acadians that year. Being thrust into foreign surroundings without family or friends would have been the worst situation imaginable for this close-knit, family oriented community.

The British thought the expulsion would rid them of the Acadians once and for all. However, they underestimated the spirit of the Acadian people and their attachment to the land they had lovingly farmed for generations. Many made the long trek back to Acadia, the place they would always consider home.

Today, Acadians throughout New Brunswick, Nova Scotia, and Prince Edward Island celebrate Christmas like no other culture in Canada. The festive season, with its rich foods, joyous music, and, most importantly, visits with family and friends, is a time many look forward to all year long. For most Acadians, midnight mass on Christmas Eve marks the beginning of the holiday season, and is an occasion not to be missed. After mass, families gather together for a *réveillon* with plenty of music and singing, as well as the traditional feast. Tables groan beneath the weight of *poutines, râpées,* and *tourtière* laid out for these late night feasts.

In addition to the sumptuous array of food, no Acadian get-together would be complete without music. At Christmas, the spoons, fiddles, accordions, mandolins, and pianos are tuned up, and the distinctive sounds of lively jigs, reels, and, of course, carols, keep toes tapping into the wee hours of the morning. While most Anglo families are crawling out of bed early on Christmas Day, Acadians are just tucking in for a few hours' sleep before the next round of visiting and feasting begins.

**An Explosive Christmas**

In December of 1916, nine-year-old Hugh MacLennan's prayers were answered when his father, Dr. Samuel MacLennan, arrived safely back in Halifax after a year overseas. Dr. MacLennan, who had shipped out on Christmas Eve the previous year, had been invalided home early due to an infection in his arm.

While Dr. MacLennan had been away, his wife, Kate, and their two children had gone to stay with her parents in Cape Breton. When she received word of her husband's imminent return, Kate hurriedly rented a house in Halifax. Hugh's sister was away at boarding school at that time, so mother and son rushed back to "the brown old town" just in time to meet

Dr. MacLennan's ship. After spending the year anxiously wondering if his father would be one of the lucky ones who made it home in one piece, Hugh was thrilled when he caught sight of his father coming down the gangplank. It looked as though that Christmas was going to be much brighter for the MacLennan family than the previous one had been.

Christmas of 1915 had been miserable for young Hugh and his sister. After watching their father march off to war, the children had gone home and hung up their stockings as usual. As MacLennan later recalled in his essay, "An Orange from Portugal": "It was a bleak night for children to hang up their stockings and wait for Santa Claus, but next morning, we found gifts in them as usual, including a golden orange in each toe."

After their joyous reunion at the pier, the MacLennan family made their way across town to their new accommodations. The minute they stepped through the front door, it hit them — the cloying smell of gas. Dr. MacLennan, an impatient, intolerant man, dropped his bags in the foyer and, grumbling about the carelessness of some people, went off in search of the leak. Hugh watched in disbelief as his father lit a match and started down into the basement. Seconds later, the house exploded.

The explosion "shook the ground like an earthquake," shattered windows all along the block, and was heard up to a kilometre away. Although the house was almost completely demolished in the blast, the only person badly injured was

Dr. MacLennan. He suffered severe burns to his hands and face, but the worst injury may have been to his ego. The day after the explosion, the local headlines screamed, "DOCTOR HUNTS GAS LEAK WITH BURNING MATCH — FINDS IT."

Hugh was mortified by the whole affair. He later declared, "I wished to God he had been able to tell his story sooner and stick to it. After all, he was a first-class doctor, but what would prospective patients think if every time they heard his name they saw a picture of an absent-minded veteran looking for a gas leak in a dark basement with a lighted match."

The MacLennans ended up spending Christmas in a single room in a Dickensian residential hotel on Barrington Street. Despite the cramped quarters, the trauma of the explosion, and the fact that he had just had his faith in Santa Claus destroyed by an older boy at school who had informed him there was no such being, that particular Christmas was one that Hugh would always remember fondly.

**White Christmas**

On December 24, 1970, Fredericton's daily newspaper reported that a "rare celestial event" was to take place early the following morning. Astronomers had predicted that the planets Venus, Jupiter, and Mars would cluster together near the crescent moon on Christmas morning. This phenomenon, which only occurs once every 800 years, was believed to have been the same one that appeared in the heavens during Christmas in 7 BC — the year of Christ's birth. In fact, astronomers speculated that this conjunction of the planets may very well have been the miraculous phenomenon known as the "Star of Bethlehem," which led the Three Wise Men to the baby Jesus. For those who follow the stars, a significant celestial event such as this would have seemed an appropriate omen in the early 1970s, a time of global turbulence and transition. And in retrospect, in the Maritime Provinces at least, the phenomenon must have seemed quite ominous.

A snowstorm had been forecast for the Maritime Provinces on December 23, 1970. Fredericton's *Daily Gleaner* predicted eight inches would fall that day. The storm would be over by Christmas Eve, they said, leaving the area cloaked in a fluffy layer of fresh white snow for Christmas Day. The prediction was not quite accurate though. The snow didn't *start* to fall until the afternoon of the 24th. And when it finally came to an end late the next day, the Maritimes were buried beneath drifts the likes of which had rarely been seen before.

Mabel Groom peered anxiously out her living room window as the snow began falling early in the afternoon on Christmas Eve. It was coming down much faster than she'd expected. She and her husband, Wesley, had planned on driving over to pick up her parents a little later that afternoon. Ever since Mabel and Wesley had started a family of their own, her parents had been coming to spend Christmas Eve with them. The suddenness and severity of this storm made Mabel nervous. She decided they should leave for her parents' place early.

As the Grooms pulled out of their driveway in Pennfield, New Brunswick, and crept along Route 1, visibility was so poor they could barely make out anything beyond their car's engine bonnet. The highway was filled with holiday travellers heading home for Christmas. The heavy traffic, poor visibility, and slippery conditions made driving treacherous. Mabel and Wesley had only gone about 10 kilometres when they rounded a corner and went into a skid. Wesley managed to pull out of it in time, but the incident frightened Mabel. She thought of the children back home with the babysitter. If something should happen to her and Wesley out there, the children would be all alone on Christmas Eve. The couple decided they'd better turn around and get home while they still could. Wesley took a back road home to avoid the heavy traffic, a move they were both thankful for later that day.

The Grooms owned and operated McKay's Motel and Restaurant, which was located right next to their house on Pennfield Ridge. When they finally arrived home after their aborted attempt to pick up Mabel's parents, Wesley headed over to the restaurant. Since it was Christmas Eve, he had intended to close early that day so the staff could get home to their own families at a decent hour. In the meantime, Mabel began preparing for a cozy Christmas Eve with just the six of them. Although she was disappointed her parents wouldn't be there for their traditional family Christmas, she was tremendously relieved that she and Wesley had made it home safely and wouldn't be separated from their own children that night. After all, with a new baby in the house, this would be a very special Christmas for the Grooms.

Shortly after he returned to the restaurant, Wesley called over to the house to tell Mabel that he'd probably be late getting home. "You had better prepare for company tonight after all," he added. A nine-vehicle pile-up had occurred just up the road, and the RCMP had blocked off the highway, leaving hundreds of motorists stranded in the small community.

Once the residents of Pennfield found out about the accident and roadblock, they forgot all about their own plans for the evening and went to work helping out those who were stranded in their community. In the spirit of the season, they generously opened their homes and businesses to the storm-stayed travellers. Phones rang all along the line as neighbours called one another to find out who had room for another guest or two. Dinners were organized, supplies and bedding were scavenged from wherever they could be found, and makeshift accommodations were set up.

At least 80 people crowded into McKay's Motel and Restaurant. Many were families with young children on their way home for Christmas. They all looked a little shell-shocked as they ducked in out of the storm, brushing thick layers of snow from their hats and coats. While the waitresses rushed around taking orders and trying to make their guests as comfortable as possible, Wesley sorted out the accommodations. Once all 12 units of the motel were filled to capacity, he offered shelter in the basement to any who wanted it. One family was sent over to the house to stay with Mabel and the children, others curled up anywhere they could find a spot in the restaurant.

The mood among the people at McKay's became a little emotional when darkness fell and it became clear that, like it or not, this was where they were going to spend Christmas Eve, and possibly Christmas Day. For some, the thought of being separated from their loved ones that night was devastating. Others found the situation amusing. The majority, however, were just glad to be in out of the storm. As the evening wore on, the mood grew more festive. Among those stranded at McKay's that night was a band from Boston. Finding themselves with a captive audience, the band members decided to put on an impromptu performance. They set up their instruments beside the Christmas tree and before long everyone was singing along.

Many wayfarers throughout the Maritimes were not as lucky as those stranded in Pennfield that night. Hundreds spent the night trapped in frigid vehicles. For one family of seven, that Christmas Eve blizzard turned into a nightmarish ordeal. Fred Kelly, his wife, and their five children spent 14 hours stuck in a drift on the Trans-Canada Highway just beyond the town of Sackville, New Brunswick.

At about 9:30 on Christmas morning, the snow was still accumulating at an alarming rate. Nothing in the area was moving but snowploughs and snowmobiles. Unable to get out and patrol their territory, the Sackville detachment of the RCMP decided to turn to local snowmobilers for assistance. They asked that the snowmobilers form search parties to help find stranded motorists in the area. The snowmobilers responded immediately. Not long after they began combing the area, one search party discovered the Kelly family. Their car was almost completely buried beneath mountainous drifts. And after spending the night in their vehicle with the motor running, all seven were suffering from carbon monoxide poisoning. Once the rescuers had dug them out, they were rushed to the hospital, where they spent the next few days recovering from their ordeal.

For another group travelling by bus from Moncton to Fredericton, Christmas Eve of 1970 was one they would not soon forget. The bus, carrying 24 passengers from the Moncton airport to Fredericton, departed at about 5 p.m. that day. Under normal conditions, the trip would have taken about two hours. However, conditions were anything but normal that day. By the time the driver ground the bus into gear and pulled away from the terminal, the storm was in full fury. As the bus slipped and skidded along the highway, ploughing through drifts almost as high as the windshield, the passengers grew nervous. From time to time, gasps and squeals were heard above the droning of the engine. After a tense five-hour drive, the bus finally spun out of control. White knuckles clutched the backs of seats as the bulky vehicle skidded sideways. The bus finally lurched to a halt in the ditch near Lakeville Corner, where it would remain for the rest of the night.

Although the passengers were a little shaken up by their ordeal, no one was hurt. Once they realized they were destined to spend Christmas Eve on the bus, everyone onboard tried to make the best of the situation. Still, most of them would have preferred to be home with family and friends rather than stuck in a ditch with 23 strangers on Christmas Eve. It wasn't until late the next morning that the passengers managed to burrow through the drifts surrounding the bus and board another that had arrived to carry them on to their destination.

In addition to those stuck in snowdrifts, hundreds of holiday travellers spent most of that Christmas stranded in train stations and airports across the region. The CN Railway station in Moncton was filled to capacity on Christmas Eve. Approximately 73 passengers spent the night on hard benches in the drafty building, singing carols and swapping stories to pass the time.

Although the great Christmas blizzard of 1970 pounded all three Maritime Provinces, Saint John and Moncton took the brunt of the storm. As the snow continued to pile up, both cities were forced to declare a state of emergency. Meanwhile, crews in all urban centres struggled to keep main arteries open for emergency vehicles throughout the holiday. In the besieged province of New Brunswick, one catastrophe followed close on the heels of the last. During the height of the storm, on Christmas Eve, an explosion rocked the chemistry building on the University of New Brunswick campus in Fredericton. It took firefighters several hours to extinguish the resulting blaze, which destroyed two floors of the building. The following day, the roof of Moncton Stadium collapsed under the crushing accumulation of snow. In addition, multi-car pile-ups and house and business fires kept emergency workers in the province rushing from one scene to the next. Tragically, at least five people in the region died as a result of the blizzard. Among the casualties was a pair of young cousins who were struck and killed by a careening taxi while walking along the side of the road near their home in New Brunswick.

On Prince Edward Island, snow began falling in the Summerside area at about 4 p.m. on Christmas Eve. By the next afternoon, 47 centimetres had buried the town, bringing everything to a halt. Midnight masses and traditional Christmas Day services were cancelled. Three- to four-metre drifts prevented everything but snowmobiles and snow-plough s from moving, and even the plods had to work hard to break through some of the more massive drifts. Electricity and telephone lines were knocked out on many parts of the Island. So, not only were Islanders left shivering in the dark on Christmas Day, most couldn't even enjoy their traditional turkey dinner — they had no way to cook it.

All in all it was a truly memorable Christmas for most Maritimers.

# Chapter 3
# O Christmas Tree

or many of us, the Christmas tree is one of the nicest things about the holiday season. Going out on the annual tree hunting expedition — whether it be to a pastoral, snow-covered wood lot or a supermarket parking lot — is often an adventure in itself. And as the first waft of balsam fir or white spruce drifts through the house, and cherished ornaments are lifted from their storage boxes and hung on the boughs, memories of Christmases past come rushing back in a flood of nostalgia.

The Christmas tree has become such an essential element of Christmas over the past century that we tend to forget it hasn't always been a part of the season. Like so many other Christmas traditions, the custom of bringing an evergreen tree indoors and decorating it has its roots in ancient pagan rituals. The evergreen tree was a symbol of life in ancient times, and during the winter solstice the aromatic green boughs were brought indoors and hung over the lintel.

It wasn't until sometime in the 16th century, however, that the first evergreen tree was brought indoors and decorated. Some credit German theologian Martin Luther with being the first person to bring a tree indoors at Christmastime. Legend has it that one Christmas Eve he was so enchanted by the sight of a small, snow-covered evergreen glimmering in the moonlight, he decided to take the tree home to show his children.

The earliest Christmas trees were actually miniature versions of those we erect today. Often, in wealthier homes, each family member had his or her own little tabletop-sized tree. These little trees were trimmed with fruits, nuts, and paper ornaments, and gifts and sweets were laid out beneath their branches.

The tradition of the Christmas tree gradually spread throughout Germany and the rest of Europe. But it wasn't until 1848, when the *Illustrated London News* featured an image of Queen Victoria and Prince Albert and their children gathered around an elaborately decorated Christmas tree, that the custom really took off. By that time, however, German and Dutch settlers had already introduced the tradition to North America.

Two years before Victoria and Albert's tree made the news, a wealthy Halifax merchant erected one of the first

A Victorian Christmas tree, ca. 1895.

Christmas trees in Canada. In 1846, William Pryor had the tree put up in his Coburg Road home. Pryor's wife, Barbara, was originally from Germany, and had grown up with the tradition. The Pryors' tree would have been attractively adorned with glass ornaments imported from Germany, cornucopias of candies, cranberry garlands, strands of popcorn, and dozens of candles. No doubt, the Pryors' tree was the talk of the town that season. And it wasn't long before the tradition caught on and spread throughout Nova Scotia and the rest of the Maritime Provinces.

In those early days, Christmas trees, with their dozens of burning candles clipped precariously to tinder branches, were extreme fire hazards. It wasn't long before people caught on to the fact that illuminating the tree with fire wasn't such a bright idea. Eventually, shiny tinsel and reflective glass balls replaced the candles. Then electricity came along and revolutionized the decorating of the tree. The strands of multi-coloured bulbs were much safer than candles for lighting up the tree. But in spite of this advance in technology, trees are still known to burst into flames every now and then.

Such was the case on December 23, 1964. That morning, the office workers at the Nova Scotia Department of Motor Vehicles in Halifax were busy finishing up paperwork before the Christmas holiday. Everyone was looking forward to Christmas Eve, when they would exchange gifts, have a few eggnogs, and go home to their families for the holiday. The office tree, a small tabletop balsam fir, had been trimmed with lights and ornaments the week before. All week long the pile of gifts beneath it had been growing steadily. Everyone agreed it was one of the prettiest trees they'd had at the DMV.

But just before noon that day, the quiet in the office was shattered when the little tree suddenly burst into flames with an audible "pouf!" A great commotion ensued as every-one scrambled to find a fire extinguisher. But there was no extinguisher to be found. Finally, someone ran to the jani-tor's closet and returned with a bucket of water, which they tossed on the blazing tree. By the time the flames were finally extinguished, the pretty little tree was nothing more than a blackened, smouldering skeleton, and the gifts beneath its branches a soggy ruin.

### The Boston Tree
Standing among the thousands of spectators crowding the Boston Common, Janette Snooks felt a surge of pride as the master of ceremonies announced her mother's name and the trim 72-year-old Aileen Dixon strode on to the stage and took her place next to the premier of Nova Scotia. It was December 4, 1988, and Aileen and Janette had been invited as special guests of McDonald's Restaurants to participate in the annu-al Boston tree lighting ceremony. As Aileen and Premier John Buchanan walked over and flicked the switch that lit up the 18,000 bulbs on the magnificent tree, the crowd roared. It was a moment Janette would never forget.

The Halifax to Boston Christmas tree is an annual tradi-tion that began in 1971, but its roots go back to 1917, the year of the Halifax Explosion. Aileen Dixon (nee Coleman) was only five months old on that fateful December 6, when the Belgian relief steamer *Imo* collided with the French muni-tions ship *Mont Blanc* in the Halifax Harbour. The resulting explosion levelled a large part of the city, killing and injuring thousands and leaving thousands more homeless. Although Aileen had not been injured, her father, Vincent Coleman, was one of those killed in the blast. A train dispatcher with the Canadian Government Railway, Coleman had sacrificed his own life in an effort to save hundreds of others that day.

The city of Boston was one of the first to respond to Halifax's plea for help in the wake of the Explosion. Their outpouring of generosity following that tragic event is something the people of Halifax have never forgotten. The Boston tree is a small token of Nova Scotia's appreciation for that aid.

When McDonald's Restaurants learned that Aileen was the daughter of Vincent Coleman, who happened to be featured on the restaurant's tray-liners at the time, the company invited her to the tree-lighting ceremony. Aileen was honoured by the invitation and by the opportunity to commemorate her father's heroic deed.

The Halifax to Boston Christmas tree is no ordinary conifer. In fact, it's arguably one of the largest, most impressive Christmas trees anywhere. The search for this perfect tree begins up to six months before Christmas. Representatives from the Department of Natural Resources comb the entire province for a balsam fir, white spruce, or red spruce that stands at least 13.5 metres tall and is perfectly symmetrical. Once found, the tree is carefully prepared for cutting. Bringing down a 13-metre conifer safely is no simple task. It takes up to four days and 25 workers just to prepare the site and the tree. First, the area around the base of the tree is cleared so that workers and equipment can get at it. Next, each branch on the tree is bound to the trunk to prevent damage. After the tree is felled it is loaded onto a flatbed truck and taken to the marine terminal, where it begins its three-day voyage to the Port of Boston. There, it is loaded onto another flatbed truck and driven through the streets of Boston, accompanied by a motorcade befitting a head of state. Once the tree arrives at the Boston Common, it is set up and trimmed in time for the tree-lighting ceremony. This joyous event, featuring perfor-mances by entertainers from both sides of the border, marks the beginning of the Christmas season for the people of both Boston and Halifax.

**The Quest for the Perfect Tree**
Some families are not fussy when it comes to choosing a Christmas tree — as long as it isn't too scrawny and will fit into the space available, with the angel on top, that's all that matters. Others, however, are a wee bit more particular. The Murdock clan from Rothsay, New Brunswick, definitely falls into the latter category. Year after year, the Murdocks would spend hours searching for the perfect tree. Because their Christmas tree always stood in the hall at the bottom of the stairwell in the family's "old barn of a place," it had to be about six to seven meters tall — a criterion that excluded all "tree lot" trees right off the bat. In addition, it had to be bushy and as symmetrical as possible — no Charlie Brown trees

permitted. The best trees, they discovered over the years, grew along the power lines.

It was a Murdock family tradition that in mid-December, Anne, Hamish, and their four children would all head out on their annual quest for the "perfect tree." So, in December of 1983, once all the children had arrived home from university for the holidays, the family piled into the Toyota station wagon and drove up to the power lines. Since it was the first time they'd all been together in a while, everyone was in high spirits as they started out. It was a bitterly cold day, however, and as they tramped over hill and dale for what seemed like hours, fingers and toes grew numb and spirits began to flag.

Finally, after what had begun to feel like a futile search, they came upon *the* tree. It was easily six meters tall, with a hefty trunk. The whole family agreed that its size and shape were *just right*. Hamish, who was just getting over a bad flu-bug, set right to work chopping down the tree. Anne and the children cheered him on from the sidelines, while stomping feet and blowing on fingers. It was growing late and they were all looking forward to getting home to a hot drink by a roaring fire.

As dusk closed in the mercury dropped even lower. The trek back to the car seemed to take forever. Once there, Hamish, Anne, and the children struggled to lift the massive tree onto the roof of their compact station wagon. But it soon became apparent to all that there was no way *that* tree was going to fit on the roof of *that* car. Anne suggested they go home and borrow the neighbour's truck and trailer and come back for the tree. But by this time it was getting dark. Having had enough for one day, Hamish decided the tree would be fine in the ditch overnight.

Driving the neighbour's truck with the trailer in tow, the Murdocks set out for the power lines around noon the next day to collect their tree. As they neared the spot where they'd left it, the thought crossed their minds that the tree might have been spirited off in the night. So when they saw that it was still lying in the ditch, a collective sigh of relief went up. They clambered out of the truck and hurried over to the edge of the ditch, eager to claim their prize. But as they got a little closer, a chorus of "Holy S---!" echoed in the frosty air. Apparently, someone *had* come along and found the tree before the Murdocks returned for it. Searching for a nice average-sized tree, they must have been delighted to discover the perfectly shaped six-metre specimen, load it onto their car, and go. Which was just what they'd done, leaving the Murdocks with nothing but the butt end of their Christmas tree.

## Chapter 4
# Old Saint Nick

or over a century, children everywhere have gone to bed on Christmas Eve dreaming of Santa sitting at the helm of a great sleigh loaded with presents, sailing across the heavens and shouting, "On Comet! On Cupid! On Donner! And Blitzen!" Santa Claus is such a familiar icon in popular culture that we often take it for granted that he's been around forever. But in fact, the Santa Claus we know and love today wasn't even conceived of until the early 19th century. Prior to that time, there were various incarnations of the Christmas gift-giver, such as Saint Nicholas and Sinter Klaas. But it wasn't until 1822, when Clement Clark Moore wrote his famous poem, "A Visit From St. Nicholas," or, as it is better known today, "The Night Before Christmas," that the figure of Santa came

into being. The poem was written as a Christmas present for Moore's six young children. And although he refers to the bearer of gifts as St. Nicholas instead of Santa Claus, it was Moore's poem that first defined the character:

> He was dressed all in fur, from his head to his foot,
> And his clothes were all tarnished with ashes and soot;
> A bundle of toys he had flung on his back,
> And he looked like a peddler just opening his pack.
> His eyes how they twinkled! His dimples, how merry!
> His cheeks were like roses, his nose like a cherry!
> His droll little mouth was drawn up like a bow,
> And the beard on his chin was as white as the snow;
>
> ... He had a broad face and a round little belly,
> That shook when he laughed like a bowl full of jelly....

Much later, an American illustrator by the name of Thomas Nast created the first visual image of Santa Claus. One of Nast's illustrations, which appeared in a book of Christmas poems in 1863, depicts the portly old fellow on the roof of a house about to make his descent down the chimney. On Santa's back is the toy-stuffed sack, and just over his shoulder is a church steeple topped with a cross. It didn't take long for merchants throughout North America to catch on to the marketing appeal of this loveable gift giver. Images of Santa soon began popping up in advertisements for all kinds of goods during the festive season.

Eventually, Santa made his way to the Maritime Provinces where, in addition to climbing down the region's chimneys on Christmas Eve, he also made appearances at stores and Christmas parties. In the late 1800s, a live appearance by Santa Claus had an effect similar to that of a major rock star appearing unannounced on our streets today — roads were blocked off, fans screamed and cried, women fainted. Back then, live appearances by Santa normally occurred only in major centres such as Fredericton, Saint John, and Halifax. Children living in outlying areas had little hope of ever seeing the mythical figure in person. Instead, they wrote letters addressed to Santa Claus at the North Pole telling him how good they had been all year and what they wanted for Christmas. Most letters to Santa were sent via the conventional postal route. However, many children in Atlantic Canada preferred to send their wishes up in smoke. Once their letters were written and ready to go, they were tossed into the woodstove in the belief that the thoughts expressed therein would fly up the chimney and be carried on the wind to the North Pole.

**Santa Arrives in Outport Newfoundland**
Back in the early days, merchants weren't the only ones responsible for introducing Santa Claus to the children of Atlantic Canada. Missionaries working in remote areas of Newfoundland and Labrador also shared that pleasure. In

## Old Saint Nick

the late 1800s, when a young English doctor by the name of Wilfred Grenfell arrived in northern Newfoundland to establish the mission hospital at Cape St. Anthony, he was shocked by the impoverished conditions he encountered. In the small, scattered settlements, people lived in rough shacks without even the most rudimentary conveniences. There were no schools or medical facilities for hundreds of kilometres, and stores were simply non-existent. All goods were bartered for. In fact, there were so few goods in the area that, according to Grenfell, many of the children of St. Anthony had never even possessed a store-bought toy.

When the Christmas season approached that year, Grenfell's thoughts turned to home and the "conventional pleasures of the season." In that remote northern outpost, where just putting food on the table was a daily struggle for most, there would be no plum pudding or holly and mistletoe, no lavish Christmas dinners or exchanging of presents. And, perhaps worst of all, there would be no visit from Santa. Although the children of Cape St. Anthony may have *heard* of Santa Claus, they certainly had no expectations of him visiting their community. As the doctor brooded on the situation, it occurred to him that it was within his means to bring a little joy into the lives of these children. Grenfell decided he would introduce Santa Claus to the children of Cape St. Anthony.

The mission soon became a hive of activity. A room at the hospital was secured for the event, a tree was picked out, and preparations were made. When the mission workers announced that Santa Claus would visit Cape St. Anthony that year, there was such a hubbub in the community that Grenfell feared there wouldn't be enough gifts to go around or enough space to accommodate the crowd that was eagerly anticipating the event.

The day before Santa was to arrive, Grenfell and his assistant were called away to tend a patient on the Straits of Belle Isle. They were travelling by dogsled, the only mode of transportation in the region at that time. And since their route that day was awash in areas covered with dodgy ice, the trip took much longer than it should have. The doctor began to worry that he would not make it back to St. Anthony in time for Santa's arrival the following day. But the next morning dawned bright and clear, and the men set out early, feeling optimistic that they might make it back in time after all.

That notion went by the wayside, however, when they met up with a man from another community seeking the doctor. He explained to Grenfell that a boy in his community had accidentally shot himself in the leg and was in critical condition. Without a moment's hesitation, the doctor changed course and rushed to the wounded boy's side. One look told Grenfell the wound was bad. He feared the child would develop blood poisoning and die if he wasn't taken to the hospital immediately. So the boy was bundled up and carried out to the doctor's sled. Once again they set out for St. Anthony.

Meanwhile, in St. Anthony, the anticipation of the crowd waiting at the hospital for the arrival of "Sandy Claws" had reached a fevered pitch. Men, women, and children crowded round the doors watching anxiously for a sign of the mythical figure and his sled. When word spread that a sled was approaching, everyone rushed out front expecting to see the jolly, bearded figure of Santa. Their disappointment was palpable when they realized it was only the doctor and his patient. But Grenfell told them not to worry; he'd seen the big man headed their way. Indeed, within minutes, another dog sled carrying the unmistakably rotund figure of Santa glided up to the front door. For the underprivileged children of that isolated community, it was a truly magical moment, one they undoubtedly cherished for years.

Wilfred Grenfell's experience of introducing Santa Claus to the children of a remote Atlantic outport was not entirely unique. Around the same time that the doctor was conspiring to have the legendary figure visit Cape St. Anthony, another missionary, Samuel King Hullon, described a similar visit to the church at Hopedale, Labrador: "At just the right moment the door opened, and in came the well-known figure of picture and story — red and furry gown, long white beard and a sack of presents." The youngsters of Hopedale were completely dumbfounded by the appearance of Santa in their midst. "The children gaze in some little awe at the portly bearded figure," Hullon recorded. "Some of them forget to say their 'nanomek' (thank you) as they clutch the parcel which he hands to them, just as children in England sometimes forget under similar circumstances!"

For Hullon, the experience of bringing such joy to these children was tremendously satisfying. "Surely one of the most lovely things in the world is to make little children happy," he wrote.

### "Yes Virginia, there is a Santa Claus"

Belief in Santa Claus is what makes Christmas magical. When our childish faith in this wondrous being is shattered, a vital part of our innocence is lost forever. For most children, this is a traumatic moment in life. Such was the case back in 1897, when eight-year-old Virginia O'Hanlan's friends told her there was no Santa Claus. Virginia, seeking reassurance in her belief, asked her father if what her friends had told her was true. His reply, "If you see it in *The Sun*, it's so," prompted her to write to the editor of *The New York Sun* asking, "Please tell me the truth; is there a Santa Claus?" The editor's reply is almost as famous as old St. Nick himself:

> ...Yes Virginia, there is a Santa Claus. He exists as certainly as love and generosity and devotion exist, and you know that they abound and give to our life its highest beauty and joy. Alas, how dreary would be the world if there were no Santa Claus; it would be as dreary as if there were no Virginias. There would be no childlike faith then, no poetry, no romance to make tolerable this existence ... the eternal light with which childhood fills the world would

be extinguished... No Santa Claus! Thank God he lives, and he lives forever. A thousand years from now, Virginia, nay, ten times ten thousand years from now, he will continue to make glad the heart of childhood.

## Special Santas

As *Sun* editor Francis Church implied in his reply to Virginia O'Hanlan, Santa Claus, the kind-hearted, fatherly figure who spreads joy wherever he goes, is the very embodiment of the Christmas spirit. Over the years, thousands of men and, on occasion, women have donned the red suit and portrayed Santa, passing out presents at parties and listening to the wishes of children who line up in malls and department stores for the chance to sit on his knee and confide in this magical being. But there's much more to the part than simply wearing the outfit. For many, like Eddie Aulenback and Victor Bernard, Santa Claus isn't just a role they enact once a year and then forget about until the next December; it's a way of life.

On January 31, 2004, Eddie Aulenback woke up in the middle of the night surrounded by flames. His century old home in Martin's Point, Nova Scotia, was ablaze. Somehow, the 55-year-old managed to make it down the stairs and out the front door with only minor burns. But once outside, he realized his most precious possession was still in the house. Without a thought for his own safety, he dashed back into the burning building. Smoke stung his eyes and flames singed his hair as he struggled through the blaze to the room where his Santa suit was stored. He had just about reached the suit when smoke and flames drove him back outside empty handed. Although losing his home and all his possessions was devastating, it was the loss of that Santa suit that Eddie regretted most.

Eddie Aulenback comes from a long line of "Santas." At least six people in the Aulenback family have assumed the role over the years, including Eddie's own father, who used to dress up for his children, as well as others. Eddie was just 26 when he first donned the Santa suit himself. He was in the mall one day shortly before Christmas when he had a revelation about Santa Claus. As he passed by the long line of children waiting for a chance to spend a few seconds on Santa's knee, he realized it would be really special if Santa went out to the children and took them by surprise, rather than making them come to him. So, dressed in the bright red suit and carrying a sack filled with teddy bears, Eddie began visiting the homes of handicapped and underprivileged children all over the South Shore of Nova Scotia. For this soft-spoken Santa, the joyous reaction of the children at his unexpected arrival has been a truly heart-warming experience.

Like Eddie Aulenback, Victor Bernard also donned the red suit for the first time in his mid-20s, and has been doing so every year since. It was shortly before Christmas 1947 that 24-year-old Victor got his first taste of portraying Santa Claus.

## Old Saint Nick

That night, he was among the audience at a Christmas concert at Alberry Plains School in PEI when one of the teachers approached him. She explained that the person who was supposed to play Santa that evening hadn't shown up, and that there were going to be a lot of very disappointed boys and girls in the audience if someone didn't fill in for him. Then she asked if he would mind playing the part.

Victor was reluctant. He knew nothing about playing Santa, he told her. He suggested she try someone else. But the woman persisted, saying he was the only one there that night who was about the right size for the outfit. Victor looked around at all the expectant faces in the crowd and thought of what a letdown it would be if Santa didn't show up. After all, he was the star of the show. Finally, he relented. The teacher rushed him backstage, thrust the red costume and a rubber mask into his hands, and told him to get dressed. The next thing Victor knew, he had a bulging sack slung over his shoulder and was being instructed to sing "Jingle Bells" as he was propelled out onto the stage.

Despite his reluctance to play the role that first night, Victor ended up repeating his performance five times that week. That was 56 years ago, and the jolly 80-year-old is still at it. Victor, who was raised in an orphanage until the age of four and then shunted from one temporary home to the next, gets tremendous pleasure out of brightening the lives of others. And to his mind, there's no better way of doing that than playing Santa Claus.

## Chapter 5
# Gifts and
# Gift Giving

he tradition of exchanging gifts at Christmas is as old as the holiday itself. Changing social values over the centuries, however, have greatly influenced the gift giving tradition. Prior to the mid-1800s, goods were not terribly plentiful or accessible in Atlantic Canada. In addition, Christmas was still viewed as a sacred holiday, so gift giving was restricted to the exchange of a few trinkets and essential items. But it was also around that time that local merchants began placing lists of "Seasonal Goods" in newspapers in the weeks leading up to Christmas. Unlike the advertisements yet to come, these lists were not usually illustrated. They simply consisted of items the merchants had in stock, such as different types of fabrics, ribbons, and hats. In addition, they invariably included items

such as "rum, spirits, brandy and gin," as well as nuts, fruits, and spices for Christmas baking. It wasn't until late in the 19th century that the commercialization of the holiday began in earnest.

In the Victorian era, the exchange of "Christmas boxes" was common among the upper classes. Still, these gifts were quite modest in comparison to the extravagance of today's Christmas gift giving. In 1853, Sarah Clinch of Boston was spending Christmas with her cousins in Halifax. Her diary entry for December 24 described the presents exchanged among the family that year: "The Christmas boxes were given out today, as tomorrow is Sunday. Mine, besides the shoulder ribbons and belt, and the six pounds from Uncle Morton, were a papeteur from Heber and a neck ribbon from Aunt Mary ... and also a pretty little almanac ..."

The gifts Sarah gave were equally modest: "I gave Uncle William a book of blotting paper, Aunt Mary a bottle of lavender, Charlotte a bottle of mignonette, Louisa a papeteur ... Miriam some velvet bracelets, Heber Laurt's 'Essays of Elia', Bella and Tory collars and the three boys neck ties." The gifts she received from home, however, were slightly more lavish: "... a large music book, a pair of shoes & stockings, velvet raw silk for my New Year's dress."

**The Gift of Freedom**
Christmas gifts aren't always tangible items. In fact, sometimes it is the most intangible thing in the world that makes the

With Sincere Wishes for

A Merry Christmas and a Happy New Year

A traditional Christmas greeting.

most precious gift. Such was the "gift" that John Burbidge of Cornwallis, in Kings County, Nova Scotia, gave his slaves on Christmas Day in 1790. Although slavery wasn't as common in Canada as it was below the 49th parallel, it did exist here. In fact, prior to the British Empire's Slavery Abolition Act in 1833, slaves were bought and sold like livestock at public auctions in Halifax.

Burbidge, a British aristocrat who had come to Halifax with Governor Cornwallis in 1749, was a colonel in the militia and a judge of the "Inferior Court of Common Pleas." He owned at least four slaves, including a woman named Faney, a teenage boy by the name of Peter, and two young girls. On that Christmas Day in 1790, Burbidge signed a declaration granting the four of them, plus, "any other children my Negro woman Faney might have," their freedom. The judge must have been in a very generous mood that Christmas, or perhaps he'd had a Scrooge-like change of heart about slavery, because not only did he set his slaves free that day, he also gave them the gift of an education and a new outfit. "They shall be taught to read, and as soon as the times of their servitude expires ... they shall be dismissed with two good sutes of aparal one fit for Sundays, one for everyday ... suteable for such servants," he wrote.

Another slave owner, Colonel Henry Denny Denson of the Mount Denson Estate at Falmouth, Hants County, wasn't nearly as generous as Burbidge. At Christmas, 1781, he gave his slaves, "Spruce and John," the amount of six shillings, "as was customary for their master."

By 1790, there was a fairly large black population in Nova Scotia. Several thousand black Loyalists had come to Nova Scotia in the hopes that life would be better there than it had been in America. Sadly, this wasn't the case. Most wound up in indentured servitude for the white Loyalists. And while white Loyalists were granted prime property in their new land, black people were forced to settle on scrappy, inhospitable land that had been rejected by the whites.

Although they had achieved a degree of freedom by coming to Canada, day-to-day life wasn't much better in Nova Scotia than it had been in the States. So, when the Sierra Leone Company came seeking settlers for a new country that was being established in West Africa, many black Nova Scotians eagerly signed up.

In December of 1791, those bound for Sierra Leone assembled in Halifax in preparation for the journey. Their fleet of ships was set to sail on January 15, 1792. In the meantime, they would be spending Christmas in Halifax. A few days before Christmas that year, they sent a petition to Lieutenant John Clarkson requesting their day's allowance of "Fresh Beef for a Christmas dinner." Lieutenant Clarkson complied with the request, ordering "the whole to have fresh Beef on Christmas Day." Although that Christmas dinner was undoubtedly frugal, it must have been a joyous affair, filled with anticipation and hope for the future.

**Gifts from the Heart**
The Great Depression hit Atlantic Canada particularly hard. For most families on the East Coast, purchasing Christmas presents was simply impossible during the 1930s. Many children received little more than a handful nuts and raisins for Christmas. If they were lucky, they'd get an orange in their stockings, or perhaps a few store-bought necessities, such as hankies, hair ribbons, or a comb. Gifts given in addition to the stocking stuffers usually consisted of handmade items, such as woollen socks, mittens, and hats, or hand-crafted toys. Despite the humble nature of these gifts, they were often treasured long after store-bought presents had been forgotten.

Among the most prized homemade gifts that Florence Cormier and her sister Bernette received during the Depression was a pair of handcrafted matching doll cradles. Even though there were six children in the Cormier family, there was always something special for each of them beneath the tree on Christmas morning. Their parents, Fidele and Elise Cormier, were both creative and resourceful. Elise was an excellent seamstress and Fidele enjoyed working with his hands. Together they created many treasured presents for the children.

Marvels of recycling, the little doll cradles were created out of wooden fruit baskets. The Cormiers owned a corner store in Moncton, New Brunswick, so there was always a surplus of these baskets on hand. One year, Fidele decided to put two of them to good use. He started by removing the arched handles from the top of each basket. The handles were then cut in two and attached to the bottom of the baskets, making perfect rockers. More handles were used to form canopy frames at the head of both cradles.

Once the basic construction was completed, Elise took over. She covered the canopies and outsides of the baskets with a bit of shirred fabric. A miniature quilt and pillow completed each cradle. Florence and Bernette were delighted when they discovered the cradles under the tree on Christmas morning. Their dolls were already tucked beneath the tiny quilts, sleeping contentedly.

**The Uniform**

Christmas 1941 found Madeline Tabner of Granville Ferry, Nova Scotia, far from home. A corporal in the Royal Canadian Air Force (RCAF), Madeline had just completed her basic training in Toronto, and had been moved to Guelph, Ontario, where she would complete her chef's training before being assigned a posting. The 24-year-old was proud to be a member of the RCAF, and anxious to don the uniform. At that time, wearing the RCAF uniform was a mark of distinction, particularly for a woman. Madeline's uniform had to be specially ordered from Toronto and she'd been waiting for it for weeks. Until the uniform arrived, she had no choice but to wear her "civvies," which made her feel quite self-conscious among her fellow trainees.

On the morning of December 24, Madeline was feeling blue. She had just come down with a bad cold, as well as a touch of homesickness. This would be her first Christmas away from home, and the thought of spending it alone in the barracks was depressing. She was contemplating the dismal Christmas dinner that would be served in the mess hall when her senior officer summoned her. The officer informed her that a generous local family had invited a few of the women to Christmas dinner at their home and asked if Madeline cared to join them. Thrilled at the invitation, Madeline immediately said yes. But as soon as the words were out of her mouth, she remembered that she had no overshoes and the ground was covered with several centimetres of snow. With her cold, she couldn't possibly leave the barracks without the proper footwear. She told the officer she would have to decline the invitation after all, explaining that she had no boots to wear.

After being dismissed, Madeline returned to the

barracks feeling more depressed than ever. She hadn't received any parcels from home yet, and hadn't been in Guelph long enough to make many friends there. It was starting to look as though a lonely Christmas dinner in the mess hall was about all she had to look forward to on Christmas Day.

Not long after Madeleine returned to the barracks, the sergeant poked her head into the room and told her there was a parcel for her at the main desk. Madeline hurried down to discover there were actually three parcels waiting for her — a large box from home, a pair of winter boots from her senior officer, and her uniform.

On December 27, Madeline sat down and wrote to her sister back home, describing the gifts she'd received that Christmas: "Gert sent me a photo of herself, Mum sent me a box of cake and cookies, the identification bracelet was from Mum and Mabel, this writing paper the kids sent. Babe Girlie and Mrs. Rippey sent me a 3lbs. box of chocolates. So I didn't do too bad. Oh yes, 3 hankies. Also got my uniform Tuesday. That was quite a gift, I think."

**The Most Precious Gift**
In the weeks leading up to Christmas, six-year-old Jessie Cameron sensed that something was wrong in the Cameron household. As usual, her mother Katie was busy cooking and cleaning. With seven children — one a newborn — there was never any shortage of chores to be done around the house. But Jessie noticed that the delicious aroma of Christmas

baking didn't fill the kitchen like it usually did at that time of year. Whenever the children brought up the topic of Santa Claus and the gifts they were certain he was going to bring, a mournful look would cross her mother's tired features. Christmas isn't just about getting presents, she would remind them.

It was 1950, and employment on Cape Breton Island was scarce. Jessie's father, Dan Cameron, had to travel all the way to the town of Mulgrave on the mainland to find work as a security guard. The Camerons lived in Glenco Station, nearly 50 kilometres from Mulgrave.

At that time, the railway was an integral part of the Cameron family's daily life. Since he didn't own a car, Dan relied on the train to get to and from work. And because the station was just a stone's throw from their house, the family had become friends with many railway employees over the years. Two people in particular that Dan had befriended were Murdock Skinner and his son Basil. Father and son were both train engineers, and often on the long trip to and from the mainland, Dan would ride up in the engine with them.

For the children, the trains that passed by the Cameron house two or three times a day were an exciting diversion from the daily routine. At the sound of the whistle blowing down the line, they would race out to watch the long procession of cars roll by. They liked the passenger train best, as that was the one that always brought their father home. In addition, the passengers often threw candies or coins out the windows to them. For John Allan, who would later become a well-known Canadian musician, the passengers were a receptive audience. A born performer, he would often step dance and pretend to play the fiddle for them as they passed by.

Like many rural Maritime families back then, the Camerons were struggling financially. With seven children to feed and clothe on one meagre salary, there wasn't much left over at the end of each month. After the birth of their seventh child in 1950, Dan and Katie found themselves in dire financial straits. As Christmas approached, the couple came to the realization that store-bought gifts would be out of the question that year. And with more to do to keep the household going than she could manage, Katie had no time to create homemade presents. The thought of the children's disappointment on Christmas morning when they discovered that Santa Claus hadn't come to their house was more than Katie could bear. She decided they had to be told before they got their hopes up. One morning at breakfast, as the children were once again speculating on what Santa would bring them, she announced as tactfully as possible that Santa probably wouldn't be coming that year. A howl of protest went up from the children. Like the rest of her siblings, Jessie was bewildered by this news. She knew they'd been good all year, so why wasn't Santa going to make his annual stop at their house?

For the next few days, the children struggled with

the notion that Santa wasn't going to visit their house that Christmas. In an effort to cheer them up, Katie reminded them that there would still be midnight mass on Christmas Eve, something they all looked forward to each year. And perhaps a special treat for Christmas dinner. But this did little to raise their spirits.

Then, just two days before Christmas, something completely unexpected happened. The afternoon train had just pulled into the station, and the children were out on the bank beside the tracks collecting the candies the passengers had tossed out the windows. Suddenly, Jessie noticed the stationmaster's son running towards them. The boy was so excited that by the time he reached them, he could barely speak. Between gasps for breath he managed to blurt out, "There's a big box just came in on the train for you people!"

Forgetting all about the candies, they dashed towards the station. John Allan, being the fastest, was the first one there. Before the others had reached the station, he and the stationmaster's son had already picked up the box and were struggling to carry it back up the hill to the Cameron house. The children couldn't ever remember receiving a parcel like this before. The excitement of it all was overwhelming.

Mere seconds after they'd wrestled the box through the door and set it down, they ripped it open. Nestled inside were seven presents, each one wrapped in glossy Christmas paper with a nametag attached. For a few moments, the children just stared at the gifts in disbelief. It wasn't long, however, before squeals of delight filled the room as the gifts were passed out and dolls, toy trains, and watercolour sets were pulled from their wrappings. When Jessie unwrapped the package with her name on it, she almost cried. Inside was a porcelain doll dressed in a long gown. She'd never seen such a beautiful doll before and could hardly believe it was hers. The children were beside themselves with joy at this unexpected windfall. It seemed Santa had received their wishes after all.

A few days after Christmas, however, Jessie happened to overhear her father telling her mother that he'd found out where the presents had come from. "It was Basil Skinner who sent them," he said. The statement puzzled Jessie. Just who was this Basil Skinner, and what was his role in the gift giving? After all, the nametags had clearly said "From Santa."

At that time, Basil and his wife Evelyn hadn't started their own family yet. And as an engineer, he made enough for the two of them to get by. He knew his friend was struggling, but had no idea how bad things were until Dan let it slip that there wouldn't be much of a Christmas at the Cameron house that year. The thought of his friend's children receiving nothing for Christmas was intolerable to Basil. He'd learned from his own father that it was better to give than to receive. Murdock Skinner was well known in the community for his generosity. If Murdock knew someone was going through a rough time, he was always the first to offer whatever help he could.

Basil, it seemed, had inherited his father's generous

nature. He decided that if *he* had anything to do with it, Santa would be paying a visit to the Cameron house that year. He recruited a friend to find out the names, ages, and interests of each of the Cameron children. After making up a list, he gave it to Evelyn and asked her to go out shopping for appropriate gifts for each of them. Delivering the gifts was easy. All he had to do was drop off the package, addressed to the Cameron family, at the station.

It wasn't until she was a little older that Jessie realized just how big-hearted Basil's gesture had been. She vowed that one day she would seek him out and thank him in person. But as fate would have it, she ended up moving to Ontario and having a family of her own before she had the chance to thank him for his kindness.

Nearly 50 years later, Jessie was at a Christmas party in Windsor, Ontario, with some old friends from Cape Breton when the subject of that long-ago Christmas came up. After telling the story about the box of presents arriving on the train, she suddenly felt remorseful that she never *had* thanked Basil. She hoped it wasn't too late. That night, after the party, she went home and poured her feelings out in a letter to the man who had brought such joy to her family that Christmas of 1950. Of all the gifts she had ever received in her life, she wrote, his was the "most precious."

**Christmas Spirit All Year Round**
Just three days before Christmas of 2003, Erica Tung was diag-

nosed with an extremely rare disease known as Langerhans Cell Histiocytosis. The disease, which consumes tissues and bones, can only be controlled with chemotherapy. Since it had been ravaging two-year-old Erica's system unchecked for some time, the doctors informed her parents that chemotherapy would be necessary immediately. However, the only hospital in the region equipped to treat her was the IWK Children's Hospital in Halifax, Nova Scotia, and the Tungs lived in Prince Edward Island. Since Erica's mom, Sandy, had just given birth to her second child, there was no way she could leave home for an extended period. She and her husband, Lewis, decided he would take Erica to Halifax, where they would spend the next six months while she received treatment.

It was a traumatic Christmas for the young couple that year. Worry over Erica's condition was compounded by financial stress. The Tungs owned and operated a restaurant in the small community of Souris. Lewis did the cooking and Sandy waited on tables. Like most small business owners, they had no safety net to fall back on in times of crisis. With Lewis away in Halifax and a new infant to care for, it was impossible for Sandy to keep the restaurant open that winter. And with the restaurant closed, she had no idea how she was going to manage to pay the bills for the next few months.

When it came time to pay the rent, Sandy approached the landlord and explained the situation, hoping he would allow her some extra time to scrape together the money. To her surprise, he seemed completely unconcerned about the rent money. "Don't worry about it," he said. "Just make sure your little girl gets well." And later, when the pipes in restaurant froze up and she had to call in a plumber, the man astonished her by refusing to take a cent for the job.

In a tiny community like Souris, little goes unnoticed by the residents for long. When the Bonsai Restaurant failed to re-open after the Christmas holidays, customers and neighbours began to worry. Although they had only lived in the community for six years, the Tungs were liked and respected by everyone who knew them. Word about Erica's illness soon spread, and before long the community united in an effort to raise funds to help out the young family. The local schoolchildren started a penny drive; the Legion held a fundraiser; the women's auxiliary of a church in Charlottetown made Erica a quilt. Even rival restaurateurs in the area began collecting for the Tungs. Sandy was overwhelmed by the outpouring of generosity.

When Erica was finally released from the hospital six months later, she and Lewis returned home to a warm reception from the community. Although the two-year-old had lost her hearing in one ear and the disease had damaged her jawbone, neck, ribs, hip, and one leg, the chemotherapy had at least temporarily halted its progression. And the doctors hoped that, in time, the damage would be reversed with steroids.

Life slowly returned to normal for the Tungs. They re-opened the restaurant, and Erica spent most of her days there with them. The sweet-tempered girl, who followed her mother around with a pad and pencil in hand pretending to take orders, charmed everyone who came through the door.

When the Christmas season rolled around again, and the *Christmas Wish Book* arrived on the Tungs' doorstep, Erica eagerly flipped through the glossy pages in search of the gift she hoped Santa would bring. She paid scant attention to the dolls, ignored the games and clothes, but stopped dead when she came to a picture of a boy and girl cooking up a storm in a play-kitchen. Here was the Christmas present of her dreams. The life-like kitchen came complete with fridge, stove, sink, and cupboards filled with dishes, utensils, and pots and pans. To Erica, it was a perfect replica of her father's kitchen in the restaurant. But when she showed the picture to her mother and said that that was what she wanted for Christmas, Sandy's heart sank. The Tungs were still struggling to catch up with the bills from the past winter, and Sandy knew there was no way they could afford such an extravagant gift that year. But how could she explain that to the three-year-old? She tried to direct Erica's attention to more affordable gifts, but the child's desire for the kitchen was unshakable. Erica lugged the catalogue around with her everywhere. When customers asked her what she wanted from Santa for Christmas, she would whip it open and point to the play-kitchen. As Christmas drew closer, Sandy worried about how Erica would react when she opened her presents on Christmas morning and found no play-kitchen among them.

Then, a few days before Christmas, a friend of the Tungs showed up at the restaurant and asked Sandy to bring Erica outside. Curious, Sandy got Erica dressed in her jacket and mittens and the two stepped out into the frosty air. In the parking lot, a circle of friends and customers stood smiling broadly. And there, in the centre of the circle, was Erica's play-kitchen. For a few seconds, the child just stared at the gift, dumbfounded. When she realized it was for her, she toddled right over and began opening the cupboards and pulling out the pots and pans. The look of joy on her daughter's face at that moment brought tears to Sandy's eyes. All that they'd been through that past year came rushing back to her, and suddenly she was overwhelmed with gratitude. She was grateful for having her daughter and husband home for Christmas. She was grateful that Erica's disease was in remission for the time being. And last, but not least, she was grateful that they lived in a community that had been there to help out in their time of need. Christmas spirit wasn't something the community of Souris adopted once a year and then forgot about for the remaining 11 months, she realized. It was something that flourished there all year long.

# Chapter 6
# Yuletide Adventures

hristmas adventures invariably occur in the wilderness, it seems. In Atlantic Canada, the wilderness has many different faces. It can be pristine and pastoral, bleak and barren, or rough and rugged. It may be brutal, harsh, and unforgiving or, just as frequently, gentle and benevolent. For those who spend Christmas in the wilderness, the holiday is often a reflection of the surroundings.

### Rosebank Cottage Christmas

In 1816, Lord Dalhousie, the governor of Nova Scotia, decided it was time the large tract of wilderness in the centre of the province was settled. Since the end of the Napoleonic Wars, the British had found themselves with a surplus of soldiers and insufficient labour to keep them occupied. Dalhousie felt the perfect solution would be to offer the disbanded soldiers land grants in the midst of the wilderness, in the hope that they would carve out a settlement. Many renounced this idea, maintaining that military men were highly unsuitable for this type of undertaking. Charles Lawrence, a former governor, was one of the biggest opponents of Dalhousie's settlement scheme. The former governor even went so far as to call the disbanded soldiers "the King's Bad Bargains." But this didn't deter Dalhousie. Determined to carry out his plan for a settlement, he appointed Captain William Ross to lead a group of 172 disbanded soldiers into the wilderness.

In August of 1816, Captain Ross, along with his wife, Mary, and four small children, and the other soldiers and their families, sailed from Halifax to Chester. From Chester, they set out on the 30-kilometre journey inland on foot. Because no one in the party owned a horse, and wagons couldn't be pulled over the densely forested terrain, the men, women, and children made the trek with all of their worldly possessions on their backs. Years later, young Edward Ross would make this journey in half a day in fine weather. But that first trip took much longer. The terrain was rough; stumbling over boulders, wading through rivers and streams, and skirting around dozens of lakes along the trail slowed the group down tremendously.

The settlers arrived at Sherbrooke (later renamed New Ross after its founder) on August 7, 1816. With winter fast approaching, it was essential that the backbreaking labour of clearing the land by hand and erecting temporary shelters be started immediately. As luck would have it, that first winter turned out to be one of the most severe on record. It was fraught with hardship and suffering for the settlers. Their hastily erected cabins were dark and drafty, providing little protection from the bitter winds and cold temperatures. And, since there were still no roads into or out of the settlement, and no horses, all of their supplies had to be carried in on the backs of the men. Given the circumstances, Christmas that year likely consisted of just another day of struggling to survive.

By the following spring many of the settlers had abandoned their claims and moved on. But Captain Ross and several others remained on the land, despite the hardships. Unfortunately, just six years after leading his men into the wilderness, Captain Ross fell ill and died. Mary Ross was left with five children to care for on her own, the youngest less than a year old.

Years later, in 1835, the settlement at Sherbrooke was still a rough outpost with a rugged, frontier-town atmosphere. By that time, Captain Ross's sons were in their late teens and early 20s. Edward, the second eldest, was 22. A keen observer, he kept a diary describing the details of daily life in the settlement.

According to Edward's diary, Christmas of 1835 was a sorry affair at "Rosebank Cottage," the Ross family home.

There were few — if any — presents exchanged, and apparently no special preparations made. On Christmas Eve, the Ross brothers started drinking rum early in the afternoon. Later that day, several neighbours and friends dropped in. "In the evening Francis and George Price, Dick and Francis Rufsel, John and Francis Baggs, George Corey, George Driscoll, Jacob Burgoyne, and Andrew Kiens were here drinking," Edward wrote. The party, it seems, quickly deteriorated into a drunken brawl: "Francis and George Price afforded the company considerable amusement for a while with their drunken pranks, at last they went home and nothing would do but Burgoyne and George Corey must begin to wrestle, from wrestling they came to fighting."

Before long, the house was in an "uproar" as several of the guests jumped into the tussle. While Edward and his brother George tried to "part the combatants," the women fainted, cried, and made futile attempts to stop the fisticuffs. Finally, Edward and George managed to break up the fight. Still, the tone of the evening didn't improve much: "At last ... peace was restored, Andrew went home in a fret and I went home with Mary. In the meantime Frank Baggs and F. Rufsel were stretched on the floor along side of the other two. After a while they all recovered but George Driscoll, and all went home, we then ate our supper and went to bed and left George Driscoll lying on the kitchen floor — thus closing Christmas Eve 1835."

According to Edward, Christmas Day at Rosebank Cottage was even more miserable than Christmas Eve that year:

Friday, December 25, 1835

Christmas day. Raining almost all day. William and Rachael dined at Mr. Walker's. We had not a morsel of bread nor a cake nor a pudding this Christmas for the first time in our lives. In fact it appeared to be a dull Christmas altogether.

## Mother Nature's Gift

Although Christmas in the wilderness can be rugged and unrefined, it can also be resplendent. More than 40 years after the drunken debacle at Rosebank Cottage, Francis Bain of Prince Edward Island experienced quite a different Christmas in the wilderness.

In many respects, Francis Bain's youth was similar to that of Edward Ross. He was born in North River, a pristine wilderness in central PEI, in 1842. His father passed away when Francis was just seven years old, leaving the boy with a great burden of responsibility. He was a bright boy, with an intense love of nature. But because he was forced to help run the family farm after his father's death, he had little time to devote to his studies. Despite the challenges he faced, Bain went on to become a respected amateur naturalist and author.

In December of 1881, Francis Bain spent Christmas Day working in the woods. His profound love of nature and delight at being out in the wilderness is evident in his journal entry for the day:

Dec. 25th & 26th, 1881

We were cutting today in a growth of tall beeches whose lofty crowns of crowded twigs were covered thick with the receptacles of the nuts. We found that there were a few nuts still remaining among them. A bright-frocked jay, his plumes showing more beautiful high up in the clear sunlight, came and fed on these. He would seize a nut between his claws and the branch on which he perched, and thus secured, pick the kernel out of it. A Linnet, with his dark red head and flaming bosom, dashed like a tiny, brilliant meteor through the grey shaft of the lofty trees where we were at work, and lost in the high arches of interlacing boughs sounded his buoyant, flute-like call-notes through the clear winter sky....

Christmas Day! The hills are white with snow, save where the dark folds of the forest wrap them up in grey and invisible green, and the newly frozen surface of the harbour a sheet of cold silvery splendor and death-like stillness ... The wind came southward today, and it is mild. The sun set over the hills of the West River amid clouds flaming with orange and crimson. How softly the purple light obscured the hills and sent its aerial tints all down the valley. The flashing silver of the frozen river enhanced the splendor, and the dark fir-clad hills folded round the lovely picture.

To Bain, the landscape appears to be one great, awe-inspiring gift — its flaming sunset, absolute stillness, and snow-covered hills wrapped up like a large Christmas present in ribbons of grey and green.

**Yuletide Tragedy**

Felix Dowsley shivered as an icy wind filled the sails, driving the brigantine out of St. John's Harbour. It was December 6, 1867, and Dowsley, an apothecary from St. John's, had mixed feelings about the journey upon which he was embarking. The Christmas season was just around the corner, and he mourned the fact that this year he would be far from his wife and children for the holiday. Dowsley had recently been appointed medical officer of the Tilt Cove copper mine on the northern coast of Newfoundland. In order for him to be in Tilt Cove in time to take up his new position, he was forced to leave St. John's on December 6, as that was the last run *The Queen of Swansea* would be making to the isolated mining community for some time. As he watched St. John's grow smaller and smaller in the distance, Dowsley fretted about the future and how he would fare in the rugged mining town on the edge of the world.

*The Queen of Swansea* was a 360-ton brigantine from Swansea, Wales. On this trip, she was loaded with 12 tons of general cargo, 73 tons of stone ballast, and most importantly, mail for the miners at Tilt Cove. Among her six passengers were young William Hoskins and his sister Grinelda, who were on their way to spend Christmas with their father, the manager of the copper mine. Shortly after leaving St. John's, the brigantine ran into a violent gale. For five days, raging seas and punishing winds battered the ship. The captain and crew struggled valiantly to keep the vessel on course, but their efforts were in vain.

Finally, just before dawn on the sixth day, she was heaved into a gulch on Gull Island, a barren rock off the coast of Cape St. John. Aware that his vessel couldn't withstand much more abuse and that it could be ripped from the ravine at any minute, Captain John Owens ordered a sailor to climb to a ledge halfway up the sheer rock face of the island and attach a line. One by one, the passengers and crew struggled up the rope to the relative safety of the ledge while the sea continued to pummel the vessel. Unfortunately, not all hands were able to make it up the rope before the waves surged around *The Queen of Swansea* and she was swept back out to sea. Dowsley and the remaining 11 passengers and crew watched in horror from their narrow perch on the outcrop as the ship, with four men still aboard, was swallowed up by the seething deep. Soaked to the bone, numb with cold and shock, and with nothing but a tattered hunk of canvas for shelter from the howling wind and driving snow, the victims huddled on the black, barren rock and prayed for some kind of salvation.

On December 17, five days after being stranded on the island, Felix Dowsley wrote to his wife, Margaret. In the letter, he described the living hell in which he found himself: "Not one of us saved a single thing but as we stood, not even a bit of bread; this is our fifth day, and we have not had a bite or sup, not even a drink of water, there being no such thing on the Island. It is void of everything that would give us comfort. It is so barren and black that we cannot get wood to make a fire to warm us. Our bed is the cold rocks, with a piece of canvas, full of mud to cover us."

Hunger gnawed at them. The cold tormented them. But worst of all was the thirst. Like the Ancient Mariner, they suffered the torment of being completely surrounded by water, but without a drop to drink. "I am famishing with the thirst," wrote Dowsley. " I would give all the money that I took with me for one drink of water." But the only relief for the intense thirst was the bit of filthy snow that melted around their feet. After five days without a drop of liquid, they lapped it up like dogs.

As the days passed with no sign of rescue, it became clear to the shipwreck victims that their chances of surviving the ordeal were slim. In a letter to Margaret, Dowsley expressed his deepest fears: "You know I was never very strong or robust. My feet are all swollen and I am getting very weak. I expect that if Providence does not send a vessel along this way today or tomorrow ... some of us will be no more, and I fear I shall be the first victim."

By December 18, Dowsley and his companions had lost all hope of being rescued. Starving, half frozen, and mad with thirst, the apothecary longed for the end to come quickly and release him from his suffering. But death did not come so easily. On Christmas Eve, as he languished in icy waters up to his ankles, and lapped up melted snow to temporarily slake his thirst, Dowsley's only comfort was to dream of home. "What a sad Christmas Eve and Christmas Day it is for me!" he wrote to Margaret in what would be his last letter. "I think I can see you making the sweet bread and preparing everything comfortable for tomorrow." He envisioned his children hanging their stockings on the mantle and hoped they said a prayer for him before going off to bed.

The following spring, the crew of a passing sealer was becalmed in the waters off Gull Island and decided to take a look around. After climbing onto the barren rock, they stumbled upon the remains of the shipwreck victims huddled together beneath the piece of ragged canvas. Carefully tucked into the coat pocket of the body of Felix Dowsley were the letters he'd scribbled out to his wife Margaret in those last desperate days of his life.

## Christmas on the High Seas

On Christmas Day, 1868, Angeline Publicover found herself in the most terrifying situation imaginable. The 18-year-old was aboard a foundering schooner in the midst of a raging gale in the mid-Atlantic. The little schooner, *Industry*, had been at the mercy of the storm for a full 14 days by that time, and the meagre supply of food and water was all but exhausted.

Having been ravaged by the storm for so long, the vessel was beginning to break up. She was taking on water so badly that all aboard believed they wouldn't survive the night. A single potato was the last edible thing found onboard. Angeline and her six male companions divided the potato equally between them for what they believed would be their last Christmas dinner. However, their tongues were so swollen from thirst that they could barely swallow the morsel of raw potato. Following the pitiful meal, they said a prayer together, shook hands, and huddled in the frigid darkness of the cabin waiting for the end.

It seemed as though a lifetime had passed since Angeline Publicover, Lawrence Murphy, Captain Lewis Sponagle, and the three crewmembers had set out on the morning of Friday, December 11 on what should have been a short jaunt from LaHave to Halifax, Nova Scotia. In favourable weather, the 88-kilometre journey would have taken less than a day. Angeline had been filled with excitement as they'd pulled away from the wharf that morning. She had never been away from home on her own before, and this was a very special trip. She had recently become engaged and was on her way to Halifax that weekend to shop for her wedding gown. Captain Sponagle had gladly agreed to give her a lift to Halifax aboard the *Industry*; he was making a run down to the farmer's market with a load of dried fish and firewood that Friday, and planned to return early Sunday morning.

December 11 was one of those typically capricious Nova Scotian days. The weather was fine and winds favourable as the *Industry* set out, but before long the wind dropped. The passengers and crew found themselves becalmed off the coast of Sambro Island. Then, a few hours later, a vicious storm blew in. By that time, evening was coming on. The driving snow made it almost impossible to navigate in the growing darkness. Not wanting to take a chance on being dashed on the rocks while trying to enter Halifax harbour blind, Sponagle decided to turn and head for home. Just as they were veering around, a gust of wind swooped down and snapped the schooner's foremast in two. One calamity followed hard on the heels of the last for the hapless vessel. As they pitched and lurched on the wild sea, the cargo and supplies onboard broke free of their lashings and began tumbling around. The group's only canister of kerosene was knocked over and spilled out onto the deck, leaving no fuel for the lanterns. Worse still was the loss of most of their supply of fresh drinking water. Once the crew managed to secure the water barrels, only two gallons of the precious liquid remained.

They were nearing the mouth of Lunenburg harbour on the morning of December 12 when the wind suddenly veered to the northwest, driving the little craft out into the open waters of the Atlantic. For the next three days, the *Industry* tossed about helplessly on the towering waves. Since the trip was only supposed to take a few days at most, Captain Sponagle hadn't laid up much in the way of supplies. So, after the first few days at sea, those scant supplies were all but depleted. The captain began rationing the remaining water and the bit of hard tack left in the stores. For the next two weeks, the passengers and crew survived on a few bites of hard tack washed down with a mouthful of water each day. It wasn't long before their strength began to fail.

On December 15, their hopes were raised when they spotted an American schooner. The two ships managed to get close enough to communicate, but the seas were so rough that a rescue attempt was impossible. The most the American captain could do for them was to give Sponagle his position and directions for a course to Bermuda before the two ships were wrenched apart. Doing the best he could with no foresail, no charts, and no stars to steer by, the captain set off in the direction of Bermuda. For a couple of days the weather turned favourable, and the group began to believe they might survive the ordeal after all. But before long, another gale blew up, dashing their hopes. This one was even worse than the last. Severely battered by wind and waves, the little vessel began to founder. The crew worked frantically to keep her afloat, manning the pumps night and day. By December 25, the situation looked utterly hopeless. Starving and exhausted, they gave up the fight.

But the *Industry* didn't go down that night as expected. Somehow, the little schooner stayed afloat for another four days. And on December 29, a cargo vessel out of Nova Scotia crossed her path. The aptly named *Providence* was en route to London carrying a load of kerosene. She was 1120 kilometres east of Nova Scotia when her crew spotted the beleaguered *Industry*. The minute he laid eyes on it, Captain Hiram Coalfleet knew the small schooner was in trouble. Her foremast was gone and her few remaining sails were in tatters. Although it appeared the ship was abandoned, he decided to check it out anyway. When they were close enough, he hailed the vessel and after a few minutes the captain and crew of the schooner appeared on deck. The heavy sea made launching a small boat impossible, so in a daring move, Coalfleet manoeuvred his vessel alongside the *Industry*.

As the wind lashed the sails and the ships pitched and rolled alongside one another, the main yard of the *Providence* became entangled in the schooner's rigging. At that moment, Coalfleet knew they might all go down in the rescue attempt. But there was no turning back. Captain Coalfleet's brother and first mate, Abel, volunteered to shimmy up the mainmast with a line and cross over on the yard to the *Industry*. The captain watched anxiously as his brother inched his way across the narrow yard. Once aboard the small vessel, Abel quickly attached the line to Angeline first. She was hauled up and over the hull onto the larger vessel. Soaking wet and weak with hunger and fear, the girl collapsed the minute she landed on the deck of the *Providence*.

One by one, the remaining survivors were hoisted over onto the rescue vessel. Once they were all safely aboard, Abel climbed up and freed the *Providence* from the little schooner, managing to swing over to his own vessel just before the two ships parted. Although the Providence sustained a great deal of damage in the rescue effort, it could have been much worse. To the survivors, it must have seemed truly providential that the cargo vessel came along when it did. Shortly after they were plucked from her deck, the *Industry* went down.

Three weeks later, on January 20, 1869, the *Providence* sailed into the port of London. After a brief stay, the survivors of the Industry managed to catch a lift home aboard another vessel. And a full three months after setting out for their weekend trip to Halifax, Angeline Publicover and her fellow survivors finally arrived back home in Nova Scotia.

**Cargo Ship Christmases**
For three-year-old Forrest Ladd, Christmas of 1893 was sensational. Despite the fact that they were onboard the cargo ship *Belmont* en route to Java, Captain Frederick Ladd and his wife Grace had managed to arrange for some special Christmas treats for Forrest. This was the boy's second Christmas at sea, and when Santa Claus showed up in person

aboard the *Belmont*, Forrest was overjoyed. In a letter to her father back in Yarmouth, Nova Scotia, Grace described the events of this rather unconventional Christmas: "Last evening Fred dressed Ralph up as Santa Claus — filled him out, and with a [manila] wig and long beard, he made a splendid one. Forrest was so excited. We had prepared for his coming by making doughnuts, etc. and had some ginger beer ready for him. Forrest asked Santa 'where he had left his rein-bow?' This morning he was awake at half past five, his delight at seeing his stocking full and a large basket trimmed in popcorn (which Willie and he had popped and strung) also full, you can imagine."

Christmas of 1893 was Grace's fifth onboard a cargo ship. She had married her childhood sweetheart, Captain Frederick Ladd, in 1886. Faced with the prospect of remaining home in Yarmouth waiting for her husband to return once or twice a year between voyages, as most other captain's wives did, Grace chose to travel with him instead.

By 1893, Grace had celebrated Christmas in such exotic locales as Wellington, New Zealand, and Calcutta, India. Most Christmases, however, were spent at sea. Her letters home to her father offer glimpses into these unusual Christmases, as well as those back home in Yarmouth. On December 23, 1886, she wrote from Shanghai: "I suppose you are all very busy preparing for Christmas. I shall think of you all tomorrow evening sitting around the dining room table, filling the stockings and marking the different parcels."

Obviously a little homesick on this, her first Christmas at sea, and half a world away from her family, she reminisced about the previous Christmas: "I remember last Christmas Eve, Fletch [the family nickname for Grace's sister, Mary] and I went into town — coming back the bus broke down. We had to walk the remainder of the way through deep mud."

Christmas aboard a vessel at sea presented numerous challenges, and Grace often had to be creative in her preparations. In 1894, the Ladds were en route to Shanghai accompanied by "the most miserable crew a Ship ever left port with." Not only was the crew incompetent, the weather had been bad since they'd crossed the Gulf Stream. Grace wrote that the seas were so rough on Christmas Eve, "I thought I would have to give up making Doughnuts."

The tradition of making doughnuts and ginger beer to leave out as a treat for Santa on Christmas Eve had begun the year before, and Forrest had been eagerly anticipating the doughnut making for days. So when Grace told him she didn't think they would be able to make them that year, he was so disappointed by the news that she decided to make an effort despite the wild sea.

Santa was once again played by one of the sailors aboard ship, disguised in the manila wig and beard. This time, however, his arrival was marked by a fanfare of flares and foghorns. In spite of the fact that that Christmas was the "stormiest" the Ladds had ever encountered, Grace still managed to prepare the traditional turkey dinner with all the trimmings, including "Christmas pudding, German sauce, Nuts, Apples, Ginger Beer."

Although her letters indicate that she seemed to enjoy many of her Christmases at sea, like most Atlantic Canadians, Grace always longed to be home for the holidays. In her Christmas letter of 1893 she wrote, "I do wish we all could spend a Christmas at home. It is not the same anywhere else to me."

# Chapter 7
# Inspirational Christmas Stories

hen it comes right down to it, Christmas is not about how many presents we receive, how perfect the tree looks, or even how tender the turkey is. It's really about compassion and good-will towards our fellow human beings. This was the principle that the miserly Ebenezer Scrooge found so difficult to comprehend prior to his enlightening tour of Christmases Past, Present, and Future. But for many, displaying the true spirit of Christmas just seems to come naturally.

**The Greatest Gift of All**

In the fall of 1996, Scott Crocker was desperately struggling to maintain a normal life. The 40-year-old junior high school principal had been diagnosed with kidney disease over a decade earlier, and by 1996 he had been on haemodialysis for more than two years. His condition, Polycystic Kidney Disease, was genetic. Both Scott and his sister had inherited the disease, which had claimed the lives of both their aunt, and their father, who had died at age 45, just five years older than Scott was then.

Haemodialysis meant three, four-hour visits to the hospital each week. So, three times a week after work, Scott made the 20-minute drive from the school in Mount Pearl, Newfoundland, to the Grace Hospital. There, he spent the next four hours hooked up to the dialysis machine, arriving home around 9:30 p.m. Between dialysis and work, Scott had little time left over for his family or anything else. Once heavily involved in sports and numerous outdoor pursuits, Scott now had no energy or enthusiasm left for such activities. Fatigue, dizziness, and a general feeling of unwellness constantly plagued him. Just getting through the day was a slog, and sheer force of will was all that kept him going. Although the fall semester was only half over, Scott could hardly wait for the Christmas holidays so he could have a few days off.

Then, at 3 a.m. on Monday, October 6, 1996, Scott received a phone call that changed his life. It was the General Hospital in St. John's calling. They had a kidney match for him. The person on the other end of the line asked if he was prepared to accept the kidney and go ahead with the transplant. It was the most terrifying yet exhilarating moment of Scott's life. Time was a critical factor. His decision to accept or refuse the donor kidney had to be made immediately. If he refused, there were many others waiting in line for it. He took a deep breath and said, "Yes!" After hanging up, he sat on the edge of the bed and shook uncontrollably for close to an hour.

The rest of the day was a blur. Scott was flown to Halifax, where he was admitted to the Victoria General Hospital and prepped for surgery. And late that night, Scott underwent the transplant.

After convalescing in Halifax for a while, Scott arrived back home in time for Christmas. It was an extraordinary Christmas for the transplant recipient. Although he was still recuperating from the operation, he felt as though he'd been given a second chance in life. While in Halifax, he'd discovered that the kidney he had received was from a child who had died in a tragic house fire. Throughout the Christmas holiday, Scott's thoughts kept returning to the parents of that child. It astonished and moved him deeply to think that in the midst of their "terrible suffering and grief," they had been selfless enough to think of others and donate their child's organs for transplant. Although he had no idea who the couple were, he felt they had given him the single most precious gift he would ever receive.

**Mission to Seafarers**
Being home, surrounded by family and loved ones, is something we all desire at Christmas. As the song goes, "there's no place like home for the holidays." But for many, getting

home for Christmas isn't always possible. Seafarers in particular often find themselves thousands of miles from home in foreign ports, or out at sea over the holidays. With no gifts, no contact with family, and often no Christmas dinner, December 25 can be the most miserable day of the year for these people.

Maggie Whittingham-Lamont knows all about the feelings of desolation that seafarers experience during the holidays. Prior to the death in 2003 of Maggie's husband, Ned, he had spent many of their 21 Christmases at sea. With her husband away and no relatives in the region, Maggie would gather up her two daughters and they'd spend the day down at the Mission to Seafarers, a non-profit organization dedicated to both the material and spiritual needs of seafarers around the world. There, they helped brighten the day for lonely mariners from other countries. When Ned finally arrived home on leave, no matter what month it was, the Whittingham-Lamonts would have their family Christmas, tree and all. This occurred so frequently over the years that one Christmas, when the girls were young, they asked if they could please have "Christmas *at* Christmas" for once.

Although Maggie knew that spending Christmas at sea or in a foreign port was often lonely, she had no idea just how miserable it could be until one year when Ned called home and mentioned that all he'd had for Christmas dinner was a tin of tuna. Having just become the manager of the Halifax branch of Mission to Seafarers, Maggie decided that from then on, the mission would put on a *real* Christmas dinner, with all the trimmings, for every sailor in port over the holiday.

Preparing dinner for 60 or 70 people is no simple task. It requires a great deal of organization and a cool head. One of Maggie's most vivid memories is that of Christmas 1997. It was one of the first years the Christmas dinner was being put on at the mission and she was really looking forward to the event. The food had been purchased, the room had been decorated, and the seafarers had been invited. Bright and early on Christmas morning, Maggie went in and started preparing the dinner. After peeling, dicing, and chopping all morning, she and her team of volunteers had the turkey all stuffed and ready to go in the oven when she realized something was wrong. The oven wasn't heating up. They changed the fuses and checked all the connections to no avail. The oven was simply out of commission. As the guests began arriving, Maggie tried to remain calm. Determined not to disappoint anyone, despite the fact that she had no oven, she soldiered on. Amazingly enough, using only the top of the stove, she and her helpers managed to put together an entire Christmas dinner for 60 people that day.

Mission to Seafarers tries to fill the void that most mariners experience over the Christmas holidays. In addition to the Christmas dinner at the mission, volunteers arrange for the seafaring men and women to get access to a phone so they can make their Christmas calls home. They also deliver

Christmas boxes filled with goodies to every person onboard every vessel in port, a task that Maggie and the other volunteers enjoy tremendously. As she says, "It's nice to play Santa Claus."

In her 10 years at the mission, Maggie has had some pretty colourful experiences during the Christmas season. Among the most memorable was the time that Willy, an Indonesian engineer aboard a gypsum carrier in port, called her up a few days before Christmas and asked her to help him obtain a pig. It turned out the gypsum carrier was heading back out to sea for Christmas, and Willy had decided that for Christmas dinner he was going to prepare barbequed pig — he'd even built a makeshift barbeque on the deck of the ship. Maggie called around and finally found a place in Dartmouth where they could purchase a whole pig. Once they got to the butcher shop, they realized there was no parking anywhere nearby and had to park several blocks away. After making their purchase, she and Willy ended up wandering through the streets of Dartmouth lugging a frozen pig, which was about 30 centimetres taller than the engineer.

Although every Christmas morning she and her daughters have to rush to open their presents in order to get to the mission in time to start dinner, Maggie wouldn't trade her Christmas tradition for any other. Bringing some joy into the lives of seafarers who are lonely and far from home during the holiday is, she feels, one of the most uplifting experiences imaginable.

**Santa Claus Ltd.**
On December 6, 1917, the largest man-made explosion prior to Hiroshima shattered the city of Halifax. The entire north end of the city was levelled in the blast. At least 2000 people were killed. Nine thousand were injured and hundreds blinded by the explosion. To make matters worse, a major blizzard slammed into the city late that night, hampering search and rescue efforts and intensifying the suffering of the thousands of victims who were trapped in the ruins. It was a tragedy of overwhelming proportions.

At the worst possible time of year, 20,000 people found themselves homeless and destitute. Many had lost everything in the blast. There was hardly a family in the city that wasn't affected in one way or another by the disaster. But those who suffered most, perhaps, were the children. Many children lost one or both parents in the explosion. Hundreds of others were separated from their parents in the chaos following the blast, some never to be reunited. Still others were wounded and convalescing in hospitals. All in all, it was estimated that 10,000 children were left homeless that December.

As Christmas approached, a cloud of melancholy hung over the city. Normal life, as Haligonians knew it, had ceased to exist. The usual hustle and bustle of Christmas shopping, concerts, sleigh rides, and skating parties had vanished. The festive lighting and window displays of years gone by were also non-existent. Almost every window in the area had been shattered in the explosion. And with an extreme glass

An illustration from the *Halifax Herald*, December 24, 1917.

shortage in the region, the windows of the buildings that were still standing had been boarded up in an effort to keep out the cold, snow, and looters. The boarded up windows only added to the unsightly appearance of the beleaguered city that Christmas.

In the weeks leading up to Christmas, just about everyone in the area was busy with the relief effort, or struggling to cope with losses. Hundreds of people were still searching for missing family members. Each day, the newspapers were filled with long columns listing missing persons, those in hospitals, and the dead. Parents made desperate pleas for information regarding their missing children, and search parties continued to sift through the ruins searching for bodies. Hospitals and makeshift infirmaries all over the city were filled to capacity, and doctors, nurses, and volunteers worked around the clock to save lives and make patients as comfortable as possible. The shelters were also overflowing, and many people were forced to sleep out in the cold. Shortages of everything, including coal, only added to the misery and hardship. People lined up for hours to receive food, clothing, and necessities from depots set up at various locations around the city. With everyone frantically trying to deal with the aftermath of the catastrophe, Christmas was all but forgotten until it was almost too late.

On December 20, however, a group of merchants and concerned citizens got together and hastily formed an organization called Santa Claus Limited. Their mandate, they declared, was to collect and distribute "Christmas cheer" to the 10,000 homeless children in the city. On December 22 the organization placed an appeal for donations in the *Halifax Herald*. The verse accompanying the appeal imaginatively summed up the situation in the city:

OLD SANTA CLAUS was sailing his aeroplane
  so swift,
When, poof! There happened something that
  gave him quite a lift;
He was passing over Halifax with Yankee
  children's toys,
And it clean upset his balance with its rattle
  and its noise.
Down, down, he tumbled madly till those
  presents out he tossed;
And they'll need them, laughed old Santa, to
  replace the ones they've lost.
And so that good old Merryman can always see
  a way
To make a
  MERRY CHRISTMAS
    out of the darkest day.

The bleak mood in the city was also reflected in the wording of an ad placed by Mahons Limited, a downtown merchant. "We're Nearing the Edge of Christmas. Let us face it bravely, even cheerfully," the ad began. After an appeal for donations for Santa Claus Limited, it continued, "And, no matter how much you are opposed to a 'celebration,' let there be something of Christmas in your own home ..."

Despite the fact that Santa Claus Limited was formed at such a late date, the organization managed to bring a little

Christmas cheer to the children who had been so adversely affected by the disaster. Christmas trees were hastily erected in all of the shelters and many hospitals throughout the city. Decorations were also strung up in an attempt to add a festive appearance to the dismal surroundings of the makeshift infirmaries and shelters. And doctors and others were pressed into service to play Santa. On December 25 the shelters all served Christmas dinner to their patrons, and the relief committee distributed food to victims who weren't staying in shelters. That day, Santa visited each and every shelter and hospital to distribute gifts to the children. One reporter for the *Halifax Herald* wrote, "At some of the shelters there was much merriment among the little folk. Added to the attractions of the tree there were games, music, songs and the children will never forget the first Christmas after the great explosion."

For many it was a bittersweet Christmas. The outpouring of generosity from all around the world in the wake of the disaster was inspiring. In a letter to Father Thomas P. McManmon, a Sister of Charity in Halifax described the city's overwhelming gratitude at the kindness shown by the United States in particular following the explosion: "The sisters in these institutions were assisted by the Rhode Island Unit [the medical unit of doctors and nurses from Rhode Island] during the two weeks following the explosion. I wish you could hear the blessings which the poor and suffering invoke on the Americans. Surely the United States is the great, warm heart of the world."

It was true that the Americans were unstinting in their generosity. As soon as word of the explosion reached Boston, relief trains loaded with doctors, nurses, supplies, and equipment were dispatched. Medical units from Maine, Massachusetts, and Rhode Island flocked to the city in the days following the explosion. And ships and trains loaded with food, bedding, clothing, and medicine continued to bring much-needed relief to Halifax.

In addition, countless charitable gestures were made by Canadian corporations, governments, and individuals alike. Ordinary Canadians donated every penny they could spare. Children from all across the country donated their allowances. Glee clubs, Girl Guides, and Boy Scouts organized funding drives to raise money for the children of Halifax. The cities and towns of Moncton, Amherst, New Glasgow, Kentville, Truro, Charlottetown, Montreal, and Toronto all sent aid in the days and weeks following the explosion. And Sir John Eaton, president of T. Eaton Company, arrived in town with a train loaded with everything from medical supplies to household goods.

On Christmas Day, a commercial traveller from Truro was seen passing out "crisp bank notes" to survivors staying in the temporary shelter at the Acadian Hotel. When questioned about his generosity, the man said that the money had come from a charitable group of people in Truro. He had been around to several shelters visiting homeless adults and children that day, an experience that moved him deeply.

"This has been the saddest and yet the happiest Christmas I have ever spent," he said.

# Bibliography

Bruce, Harry. *An Illustrated History of Nova Scotia.* Halifax: Nimbus Publishing, 1997.

Cameron, Elspeth. *Hugh MacLennan: A Writer's Life.* Toronto: U of T Press, 1981.

Cameron, Elspeth, ed. *The Other side of Hugh MacLennan: Selected Essays Old and New.* Toronto: Macmillan, 1978.

Campbell, Sabine, ed.*Home for Christmas: Stories from the Maritimes & Newfoundland.* Fredericton: Goose Lane Editions, 1999.

Choyce, Lesley. *The Coasts of Canada: A History.* Fredericton: Goose Lane Editions, 2002.

Creighton, Helen. *A Life in Folklore.* Toronto: McGraw-Hill Ryerson Limited, 1975.

Fortier, L.M. *Champlain's Order of Good Cheer.* Toronto: Thomas Nelson & Sons Ltd., 1928.

# Bibliography

Galgay, Frank and Michael McCarthy, eds. *A Christmas Box.* St. John's: Harry Cuff Publications Ltd., 1998.

Ganong, William Francis. *Champlain's Island.* Saint John: The New Brunswick Museum, 2003.

Glasner, Joyce. *The Halifax Explosion: Surviving the Blast that Shook a Nation.* Canmore: Altitude Publishing, 2003.

Hallett, Meghan, ed. *The Dairy of Sarah Clinch: A Spirited Socialite in Victorian Nova Scotia.* Halifax: Nimbus Publishing, 2001.

Leopold, Caroline. *The History of New Ross in the County of Lunenburg Nova Scotia, 1971.* Copyright Canada, 1971.

MacMechan, Archibald. *Sagas of the Sea.* Toronto: J.M. Dent & Sons Ltd., 1923.

McCarthy, Mike and Alice Lannon, eds. *Yuletide Yarns: Stories of Newfoundland and Labrador Christmases Gone By.* St. John's: Creative Press, 2002.

Nichols, Louise, ed. *Quite a Curiosity: The Sea Letters of Grace F. Ladd.* Halifax: Nimbus Publishing, 2003.

Sider, Gerald M. *Mumming in Outport Newfoundland*. Toronto: New Hogtown Press, 1977.

Simpson, Ann, ed. *An Orange From Portugal: Christmas Stories from the Maritimes and Newfoundland*. Fredericton: Goose Lane Editions, 2003.

Stevens Bunning, Patricia. *Merry Christmas: A History of the Holiday*. New York: MacMillan Publishing Co. Inc., 1979.

Weale, David. *An Island Christmas Reader*. Charlottetown: Acorn Press, 1994.

# Photo Credits

**Cover:** Nova Scotia Archives; Collection of Joyce Glasner: page 64; Glenbow Archives NA-1194-4: page 28; *Halifax Herald*: page 104; Public Archives and Records Office of Prince Edward Island, H. B. Sterling Fonds, H. B. Sterling, Accession #3218/184: page 45.

# Acknowledgements

I am grateful to the many people who graciously shared their memories and stories with me for this book. Heartfelt thanks to Ruth Skinner, Jessie Daye, Anne Murdock, Elspeth Murdock-Knickerson, Wesley and Mabel Groom, Florence Kingston, Sandy Tung, Eddie Aulenback, Victor Bernard, Ron Barkhouse, Madeline Secord, Scott Crocker, Janette Snooks, Maggie Whittingham-Lamont, and Liam Warner. I am also indebted to all those who offered suggestions, information, and encouragement along the way. Many thanks to Valerie Poirier, Dave Knickerson, Claudia Kingston, Josephine Walsh-Mahaux, and Sandra Phinney.

I would also like to thank the staff and volunteers at the Provincial Archives of Nova Scotia, the Provincial Archives of New Brunswick, the Provincial Archives of Prince Edward Island, the New Ross Historical Society, and the Yarmouth County Museum and Archives for their assistance.

Thank you to Kara Turner, Altitude Publishing's associate publisher, for her valuable suggestions. And to my editor, Jill Foran, for her careful reading and insightful suggestions, which greatly improved the manuscript.

Last but not least, this book would not have been possible without the constant support, encouragement, and understanding of my husband, Doug.

Quotes contained in this book were obtained from the following sources: *A Christmas Box,* editors Frank Galgay and Michael McCarthy; *Champlain's Order of Good Cheer,* L.M. Fortier; *Champlain's Island,* William Francis Ganong; *Yuletide Yarns: Stories of Newfoundland and Labrador Christmases Gone By,* editors Mike McCarthy and Alice Lannon; *The Other Side of Hugh MacLennan: Selected Essays Old and New; The Halifax Herald*; the dairy of Sarah Clinch in the Provincial Archives of Nova Scotia; the diary of Edward Ross in the Ross Farm Museum archives; the Grace Ladd letters in the Yarmouth County Museum and Archives; the diary of Francis Bain in the Provincial Archives of Prince Edward Island.

# About the Author

Joyce Glasner lives in Halifax, Nova Scotia. Her articles on gardening, travel, and the arts have appeared in a variety of publications. Her first book, *The Halifax Explosion: Surviving the Blast that Shook a Nation*, was published by Altitude in 2003.

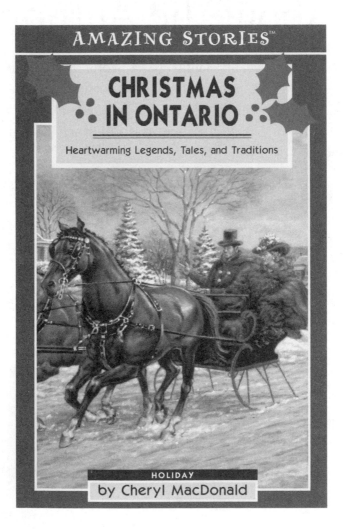

AMAZING STORIES™

# CHRISTMAS IN ONTARIO

Heartwarming Legends, Tales, and Traditions

HOLIDAY

by Cheryl MacDonald

ISBN 1-55153-779-6

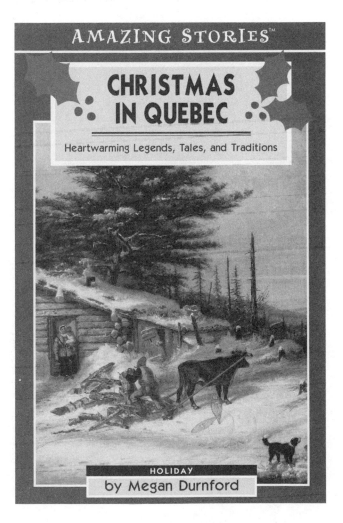

ISBN 1-55153-784-2

AMAZING STORIES™

CHRISTMAS IN
THE PRAIRIES

Heartwarming Legends, Tales, and Traditions

HOLIDAY
by Rich Mole

ISBN 1-55153-782-6

ISBN 1-55153-786-1

# OTHER AMAZING STORIES

These titles are available wherever you buy books. If you have trouble finding the book you want, call the Altitude order desk at 1-800-957-6888, e-mail your request to: orderdesk@altitudepublishing.com or visit our Web site at www.amazingstories.ca

New AMAZING STORIES titles are published every month.